CAMBRIDGE LIBRARY COLLECTION

Books of enduring scholarly value

Literary Studies

This series provides a high-quality selection of early printings of literary works, textual editions, anthologies and literary criticism which are of lasting scholarly interest. Ranging from Old English to Shakespeare to early twentieth-century work from around the world, these books offer a valuable resource for scholars in reception history, textual editing, and literary studies.

Studies of a Biographer

Sir Leslie Stephen (1832–1904) was founding Editor of the *Dictionary of National Biography (DNB)*. Also a writer on philosophy, ethics, and literature, he was educated at Eton, King's College, London, and Trinity Hall, Cambridge, where he remained as a Fellow and a tutor for a number of years. Though a sickly child, he later became a keen and successful mountaineer, taking part in first ascents of nine peaks in the Alps. These biographical essays and critiques were written originally for the *National Review* and published as two two-volume sets in 1898 and 1902. These vignettes show that, despite the years of preparing material for the *DNB* to its particular editorial requirements, Stephen was still a master of the finely crafted depiction of the essence of his chosen subjects. Volume 1 includes a consideration of the art of biography, a critique of works on Johnson, and essays on Gibbon and Wordsworth.

T0371118

Cambridge University Press has long been a pioneer in the reissuing of out-of-print titles from its own backlist, producing digital reprints of books that are still sought after by scholars and students but could not be reprinted economically using traditional technology. The Cambridge Library Collection extends this activity to a wider range of books which are still of importance to researchers and professionals, either for the source material they contain, or as landmarks in the history of their academic discipline.

Drawing from the world-renowned collections in the Cambridge University Library and other partner libraries, and guided by the advice of experts in each subject area, Cambridge University Press is using state-of-the-art scanning machines in its own Printing House to capture the content of each book selected for inclusion. The files are processed to give a consistently clear, crisp image, and the books finished to the high quality standard for which the Press is recognised around the world. The latest print-on-demand technology ensures that the books will remain available indefinitely, and that orders for single or multiple copies can quickly be supplied.

The Cambridge Library Collection brings back to life books of enduring scholarly value (including out-of-copyright works originally issued by other publishers) across a wide range of disciplines in the humanities and social sciences and in science and technology.

Studies of a Biographer

VOLUME 1

LESLIE STEPHEN

CAMBRIDGE
UNIVERSITY PRESS

CAMBRIDGE UNIVERSITY PRESS

Cambridge, New York, Melbourne, Madrid, Cape Town,
Singapore, São Paolo, Delhi, Mexico City

Published in the United States of America by Cambridge University Press, New York

www.cambridge.org
Information on this title: www.cambridge.org/9781108047692

© in this compilation Cambridge University Press 2012

This edition first published 1898
This digitally printed version 2012

ISBN 978-1-108-04769-2 Paperback

STUDIES OF A BIOGRAPHER

STUDIES OF
A BIOGRAPHER

By LESLIE STEPHEN

VOL. I

LONDON

DUCKWORTH and CO.

3 HENRIETTA STREET, W.C.

1898

Edinburgh : T. and A. CONSTABLE, Printers to Her Majesty

I HAVE to acknowledge with many thanks the permission of the proprietors of the *National Review* (in which most of the following articles appeared), of the *Fortnightly Review*, and of the *Cornhill Magazine*, to republish these studies.

LESLIE STEPHEN.

June 1898.

CONTENTS

STUDIES OF A BIOGRAPHER

NATIONAL BIOGRAPHY

MR. SIDNEY LEE has recently (February 1896) delivered at the Royal Institution a lecture upon National Biography. No one has a better right to speak upon the subject. He has been sole editor of the later volumes of the *Dictionary of National Biography*, and, as I can testify, had a very important share in preparing every previous volume. He spoke, therefore, from considerable experience, and if I were to deal with his subject from the same point of view, I should have little more to do than say 'ditto' to most of his remarks. I would not contradict even his statistics, although, as a matter of fact, they differ to some extent from my own calculations—I put that down to the known perversity of arithmetic in general. But I also think that in dealing briefly with a large subject, he left untouched certain considerations which are a necessary complement to his argument. I shall venture from this point of view to say something of a matter in which I have some personal interest.

When the old *Biographia Britannica* was coming out, Cowper made the unpleasant remark that it was

> A fond attempt to give a deathless lot
> To names ignoble, born to be forgot.

If that was a fair judgment, what are we to say to the modern work, which includes thousands of names too obscure for mention in its predecessor? When Mr. Lee speaks of the 'commemorative instinct' as justifying his undertaking, the enemy replies that a very small minority of the names deserve commemoration. To appeal to instinct is to repudiate reason and to justify monomania. Admitting, as we all admit, the importance of keeping alive the leading names in history, what is the use of this long procession of the hopelessly insignificant? Why repeat the familiar formula about the man who was born on such a day, was 'educated at the grammar school of his native town,' graduated in such a year, became fellow of his college, took a living, married, published a volume of sermons which nobody has read for a century or two, and has been during all that time in his churchyard? Can he not be left in peace, side by side with the 'rude forefathers of the hamlet,' who are content to lie beneath their quiet mounds of grass? Is it not almost a mockery to persist in keeping up some faint and flickering image of him aboveground? There is often some good reading to be found in country church-yards; but, on the whole, if one had to choose, one would perhaps rather have the good old timber crosspiece, with 'afflictions sore long time he bore,' than the ambitious monuments where History and its attendant cherubs are eternally poring over the list of the squire's virtues and honours. Why struggle against the inevitable? Better oblivion than a permanent admission that you were thoroughly and hopelessly commonplace. I confess that I sometimes thought as much when I was toiling on my old treadmill, now Mr. Lee's. Much of the work to be done was uninteresting, if not absolutely repulsive. I was often inclined to sympathise with the worthy Simon Browne, a Nonconformist divine of the last century. Poor Browne had received a terrible shock. Some accounts say that he had lost his wife and only son; others that he had 'accidentally strangled a highwayman,'—not, one would think, so painful a catastrophe. Anyhow, his mind became affected;

he fancied that his 'spiritual substance' had been annihilated; he was a mere empty shell, a body without a soul; and, under these circumstances, as he tells us, he took to an employment which did not require a soul : he became a dictionary-maker. Still, we should, as he piously adds, 'thank God for everything, and therefore for dictionary-makers.' Though Browne's dictionary was not of the biographical kind, the remark seemed to be painfully applicable. Browne was only giving in other words the pith of Carlyle's constant lamentations when struggling amidst the vast dust-heaps accumulated by Dryasdust and his fellows. Could any good come of these painful toilings among the historical 'kitchen middens'? If here and there you disinter some precious coin, does the rare success repay the endless sifting of the gigantic mounds of shot rubbish? And yet, by degrees, I came to think that there was really a justification for toils not of the most attractive kind. When our first volume appeared, one of our critics complained of me for not starting with a preface. A preface saves much trouble to a reviewer—sometimes the whole trouble of reading the book. I do not, however, much regret the omission, for the real utility of our undertaking, as it now presents itself to my mind, had not then become fully evident. I am not about to write a preface now, but I wish to give a hint or two of what I might or ought to have said in such a performance had I clearly perceived what has been gradually forced upon me by experience.

The 'commemorative instinct' to which Mr. Lee refers has, undoubtedly, much to do with the undertaking ; but, like other instincts, it requires to be regulated by more explicit reason. The thoroughbred Dryasdust is a very harmless, and sometimes a very amiable, creature. He may urge that his hobby is at least a very innocent one, and that we have no more call to condemn a man who has a passion for vast accumulations of dates, names, and facts than to condemn another for a love of art or natural history. The specialist who is typified in O. W. Holmes's *Scarabee*, the man who devotes a lifetime to acquiring abnormal familiarity with the minutest peculiarities of some obscure tribe of insects, does no direct harm to his fellows, and incidentally contributes something, however minute the contribution may be, to scientific progress. We must respect the zeal which enables a man to expend the superabundant energy, which might have led to fame or fortune,

upon achievements of which, perhaps, not half
a dozen living men will appreciate either the
general value or the cost to the worker.   Dryasdust deserves the same sort of sympathy.   He has,
no doubt, his weaknesses.   His passion becomes a
monomania.   He spends infinite toil upon work
which has no obvious interest, and he often comes
to attach an absurd importance to his results.
Such studies as genealogy or bibliography have
but a remote bearing upon any of the vital problems
suggested by the real historian.   We shudder
when we read that the excellent Colonel Chester
spent years upon investigating the genealogy of
Washington, and accumulated, among many other
labours, eighty-seven folio volumes, each of more
than 400 pages of extracts from parish registers.
He died, it is added, of 'incessant work.'   The
late Mr. Bradshaw, again, a man of most admirable character, and very fine intellectual qualities,
acquired, by unremitting practice, an astonishing
power of identifying at a glance the time and
place of printing of old books.   He could
interpret minute typographical indications as the
Red Indian can read on a dead leaf or blade of
grass the sign of the traveller who made it.
Certainly one is tempted to regret at first sight

that such abilities were not applied in more obviously useful fields. What do we care whether one or another obscure country squire in the sixteenth or seventeenth century had the merit of being progenitor of Washington? Can it really matter whether a particular volume was printed at Rotterdam or at Venice—in the year 1600 or ten years sooner or later? I will not discuss the moral question. At any rate, one may perhaps urge, it is better than spending brain-power upon chess problems, which is yet an innocent form of amusement. Such a labourer may incidentally provide data of real importance to the political or literary historian : he reduces, once for all, one bit of chaos to order, and helps to raise the general standard of accurate research. He is pretty certain to confer a benefit, if not a very important benefit, upon mankind ; whereas, if he fancied himself a philosopher, he might be wasting his labour as hopelessly as in squaring the circle. He is at least laying bricks, not blowing futile soap-bubbles.

The labours of innumerable inquirers upon obscure topics have, as a matter of fact, accumulated vast stores of knowledge. A danger has shown itself that the historian may be overwhelmed by the bulk of his materials.   A century or two ago we were content with histories after the fashion of Hume.   In a couple of years he was apparently not only to write, but to accumulate the necessary knowledge for writing, a history stretching from the time of Julius Cæsar to the time of Henry VII.   A historian who now does his work conscientiously has to take about the same time to narrate events as the events themselves occupied in happening.   Innumerable sources of knowledge have been opened, and he will be regarded as superficial if he does not more or less avail himself of every conceivable means of information.   He cannot be content simply with the old chroniclers or with the later writers who summarised them.   Ancient charters, official records of legal proceedings, manor rolls, and the archives of towns have thrown light upon the underlying conditions of history.   Local historians have unearthed curious facts, whose significance is only beginning to be perceived.   Calendars of State papers enable us to trace the opinions of the great men who were most intimately concerned in the making of history.   The despatches of ambassadors occupied in keenly watching contemporary events have been partly printed, and still lie in vast masses at Simancas and Venice and the Vatican. The Historical Manuscripts Commission has made known to us something of the vast stores of old letters and papers which had been accumulating dust in the libraries of old country mansions. When we go to the library of the British Museum, and look at the gigantic catalogue of printed books, and remember the huge mass of materials which can be inspected in the manuscript department, we—I can speak for myself at least—have a kind of nightmare sensation. A merciful veil of oblivion has no doubt covered a great deal. Yet we may feel inclined to imagine that no fact which has happened within the last few centuries has been so thoroughly hidden that we can be quite sure that it is irrecoverable. Over two centuries ago a lad unknown to fame wrote a thesis in a Dutch University. I stumbled upon it one day and discovered a biographical date of the smallest conceivable interest to anybody. But it gives one a queer shock when one realises that even so trumpery and antiquated a document has not been allowed to find its way to oblivion. Happily some University theses have been lost, but as the process of commemorating proceeds with accelerated rapidity, it almost seems as though we had made up our minds that nothing was ever to be forgotten.

It may be doubted whether this huge accumulation of materials has been an unmixed benefit to history. Undoubtedly we know many things much more thoroughly than our ancestors. Still, in reading, for example, the later volumes of Macaulay or Froude, we feel sometimes that it is possible to have too much State-paper. The main outlines, which used to be the whole of history, are still the most important, and instead of being filled up and rendered more precise and vivid, they sometimes seem to disappear behind an elaborate account of what statesmen and diplomatists happened to think about them at the time —and, sometimes, what such persons thought implied a complete misconception of the real issues. But in any case one conclusion is very obvious, namely, that with the accumulation of material there should be a steady elaboration of the contrivances for making it accessible. The growth of a great library converts the library into a hopeless labyrinth, unless it is properly catalogued as it grows. To turn it to full account, you require not only a catalogue, but some kind of intelligent guide to the stores which it contains.

You are like a man wandering in a vast wilderness, which is springing up in every direction with tropical luxuriance; and you feel the necessity of having paths carried through it upon some intelligible system which will enable you to find your way to the required place and tell you in what directions further research would probably be thrown away.

Now it is to this want, or to provide the means of satisfying one part of this want, that the dictionary is intended in the first place to correspond. It ought to be—it is not for me to say how far it has succeeded in becoming—an indispensable guide to persons who would otherwise feel that they were hewing their way through a hopelessly intricate jungle. Every student ought, I will not say to have it in his library, but to carry it about with him (metaphorically speaking) in his pocket. It is true that, in a physical sense, it is rather large for that purpose, though fifty or sixty volumes represent but a small fragment of a decent library; but the judicious person can always manage to have it at hand. And then, though in its first intention it should be useful as an auxiliary in various researches, I shall venture to assert that it may also be not only

useful for the more exalted purpose of satisfying
the commemorative instinct, but—I do not fear
to say so, though my friends sometimes laugh at
my saying—it may turn out to be one of the most
amusing works in the language.

I will start, however, by saying something of
the assertion which is more likely to meet with
acceptance. The utility of having this causeway
carried through the vast morass of antiquarian
accumulation is obvious in a general way. The
remark, however, upon which Mr. Lee has insisted, indicates a truth not quite so clearly recognised as might be desirable. The provinces of
the historian and the biographer are curiously
distinct, although they are closely related. History
is of course related to biography inasmuch as most
events are connected with some particular person.
Even the most philosophical of historians cannot
describe the Norman Conquest without reference
to William and to Harold. And, on the other
side, every individual life is to some extent an
indication of the historical conditions of his time.
The most retired recluse is the product at least of
his parents and his schooling, and is affected by
contemporary thought. And yet, the curious
thing is the degree in which this fact can be

ignored on both sides. If we look at any of the ordinary collections of biographical material, we shall constantly be struck by the writer's unconsciousness of the most obvious inferences. He will mention a fact which in the hands of the historian might clear up a political problem, or which may be strikingly characteristic of the social conditions of the time, without, as Mr. Herbert Spencer would say, noting the ' necessary implication.' A contemporary of course takes things for granted which we see to be exceptional; or he may supply, without knowing it, evidence that will be useful in settling a controversy which has not yet come to light. In the ordinary books such facts, again, have often been repeated mechanically, and readers are not rarely half asleep when they look at their manual. Thus I have sometimes noticed that a man may be in one sense a most accomplished biographer; that is, that he can tell you off-hand a vast number of facts, genealogical, official, and so forth, and yet has never, as we say, put two and two together. I have read lives giving minute details about the careers of authors, which yet prove unmistakably that the writers had no general knowledge of the literature of the period. A man will know every fact about all the people mentioned, say, in Boswell, and yet have no conception of the general position of Johnson, or Burke, or Goldsmith in English literature. He seems to have walked through a great gallery blindfold, or rather with some strange affection of the eyes which enabled him to make a catalogue without receiving any general impression of the pictures. The great Mr. Sherlock Holmes has insisted upon the value of the most insignificant facts: and if Mr. Holmes had turned his mind to history instead of modern criminal cases, he would have found innumerable little incidents which only require to be skilfully dovetailed together to throw a new light upon many important questions. More can be done by the man of true historical imagination—the man who appreciates the great step made by Scott when he observed that our ancestors were once as really alive as we are now— and who finds in those countless neglected and apparently barren facts, vivid illustrations of the conditions of life and thought of our predecessors. We all know how Macaulay, with his love of castle-building, found in obscure newspapers and the fugitive literature of the period the materials for a picture which, with whatever shortcomings, was at least incomparably brilliant and lifelike. Now,

the first office of the biographer is to facilitate what
I may call the proper reaction between biography
and history ; to make each study throw all possible
light on the other ; and so to give fresh vitality to
two different lines of study, which, though their
mutual dependence is obvious, can yet be divorced
so effectually by the mere Dryasdust. And this
remark supplies a sufficient answer to one question
which has often been put to me. What entitles a
man to a place in the dictionary ? Why should it
include 30,000 instead of 3000 or 300,000 names ?
Mr. Lee has given an answer which is, I think,
correct in its proper place ; but, before referring to
it, I must point out that there is another, and what
would be called a more ' objective ' criterion which
necessarily governs the solution in the first instance.
In order, that is, to secure the proper correlation
between the biographer and the historian, it is
plainly necessary to include every one who is
sufficiently noticed in the ordinary histories to
make some further inquiry probable. To give the
first instance that occurs, Macaulay tells a very
curious story about a certain intrigue which led
to the final abolition of licensing the Press in
England. The fact itself is one of great interest
in the history of English literature. The two

people chiefly concerned were utterly obscure:
Charles Blount and Edmund Bohun necessarily
vanish from Macaulay's pages as soon as they have
played their little drama. But it is natural to
inquire what these two men otherwise were, who
were incidentally involved in a really critical turning-point. A reference to the dictionary will not
only answer the question, but help to make more
distinct the conditions under which English writers
won a most important privilege. The historian
can only deal with the particular stage at which an
obscure person emerges into public, but the significance of the event may start out more vividly
when we can trace his movements below the
surface. Now to help in this search the biographer has before him an immense mass of
material already partially organised. Nobody
who has dipped into the subject is ignorant of the
immense service rendered by Anthony a Ward in
the famous *Athenæ Oxonienses*. It gives brief,
but very shrewd, accounts of all men connected
with Oxford, and records the results of a laborious
personal inquiry during his own period, which,
but for him, would have been forgotten. For the
same period we have all the collections due to the
zeal of various religious sects; the lives of the

Nonconformists ejected in 1662 ; the opposition work upon the 'sufferings of the clergy' under the Commonwealth; the lives of the Jesuits who were martyred by the penal laws; and the lives of the Quakers, who have always been conspicuous for preserving records of their brethren. Besides these, there are, of course, many old biographical collections, including the dictionaries devoted to some special class—the artists, the physicians, the judges, the admirals, and so forth. The first simple rule, therefore, is that every name which appears in these collections has at least a presumptive right to admission. An ideal dictionary would be a complete codification or summary of all the previously existing collections. It must aim at such an approximation to that result as human frailty will permit ; in other words, it is bound first to include all the names which have appeared in any respectable collection of lives, and, in the next place, to supplement this by including a great many names which, for one reason or another, have dropped out, but which appear to be approximately of the same rank. The rule, it is obvious, must be in part the venerable 'rule of thumb,' but it gives a kind of test which is a sufficient guide in discreet hands.

The advantage of this does not, I hope, require much exposition. I will only make one remark. Every student knows the vast difference which is made when you have some right to assume the completeness of any research. I may look into books, and search libraries on the chance of finding information indefinitely. But if I have a book or a library of which I can say with some confidence that, if it is not there, the presumption is that it does not exist, my labour has a definite, even though it be a negative, result. That, for example, is the sufficient justification of the collection of every kind of printed matter in the British Museum. It is not only that nobody can say beforehand what bit of knowledge may not turn out to be useful, but that one has the immense satisfaction of knowing that a fact not recorded somewhere or other on those crowded shelves must be, in all probability, a fact for which it is idle to search further. No biographical dictionary can be in the full sense exhaustive ; an exhaustive dictionary would involve a reprint of all the parish registers, to mention nothing else ; but it may be approximately exhaustive for the purposes of all serious students of any of the various departments of history. In a great number of cases, moreover, this can be achieved with a tolerable approximation to completeness. We take, for example, any of the more important names around which has been raised a lasting dust of controversy. A dictionary ought, in the first place, to supply you with a sufficient indication of all that has been written upon the subject; it should state briefly the result of the last researches; explain what appears to be the present opinion among the most qualified experts, and what are the points which seem still to be open; and, above all, should give a full reference to all the best and most original sources of information. The most important and valuable part of a good dictionary is often that dry list of authorities which frequently costs an amount of skilled labour not apparent on the surface, and not always, it is to be feared, recognised with due gratitude. The accumulation of material makes this a most essential part of the work; for we are daily more in want of a guide through the wilderness, and a judicious indication of the right method of inquiry gives often what it may be hard to find elsewhere, and is always a useful check upon our unassisted efforts. When you plunge into the antiquarian bog you are glad to have signposts, showing where previous adventurers have been engulphed; where some sort of feasible track has been constructed, and who are the trustworthy guides. Moreover, for a vast variety of purposes, the dictionary, though only second-hand authority, may be quite sufficient for all that is required. In following any of the countless tracks that may lead through history, you meet at every step with persons and events intruding from different regions. The man of letters may be affected by a political intrigue; a soldier may come into contact with men whose chief activity belongs to literature or science. The most thoroughgoing inquirer has to take a vast number of collateral facts upon trust; and it may save him infinite trouble to get the results of special knowledge upon what are to him collateral points.

This, to which I might add indefinitely, corresponds to what I may call the utilitarian aspect of a dictionary: the immediate purpose to which it may be turned to account by students in any historical inquiry. It should be a confidential friend constantly at their elbow, giving them a summary of the knowledge of antiquaries, genealogists, bibliographers, as well as historians, upon every collateral point which may happen for the moment to be relevant. But, so far, however well done, it must be admitted that it is bound to be rather dry. To be reduced to a specimen put in a museum is not a very cheering prospect, and offers little satisfaction for the commemorative instinct. Now I have to add that within certain limits the dictionary may be of importance in that direction too. I do not expect that a future Nelson will exclaim, 'Victory, or an article in *The Biographical Dictionary*!' I have never found my own appetite for labour stimulated by the flattering hope that I might some day be the subject instead of the author of an article. If I thought that my posthumous wishes would be respected, I should beg to be omitted from the supplement. But, for all that, the dictionary article may do much to keep alive the memory of people whom it is good to remember. Nobody will expect the poor dictionary-maker to be a substitute for Boswell or Lockhart. The judicious critic is well aware that it is not upon the lives of the great men that the value of the book really depends. It is the second-rate people—the people whose lives have to be reconstructed from obituary notices, or from references in memoirs and collections of letters; or sought in prefaces to posthumous works; or sometimes painfully dug out of collections of manuscripts, and who really become generally accessible through the dictionary alone—that provide the really useful reading.   There are numbers of such people whom one first discovers to be really interesting when the scattered materials are for the first time pieced together.   Nobody need look at Addison or Byron or Milton in a dictionary.   He can find fuller and better notices in every library; and the biographer must be satisfied if he has put together a useful compendium of all the relevant literature.   The conditions of his work are sufficiently obvious, and of course exclude anything like rhetoric or disquisition in criticism.   He may indicate but cannot expatiate.   He has before him an ideal which he very well knows is never quite realised.   Condensation is not only the cardinal virtue of his style, but the virtue to which all others must be sacrificed.   He must be content sometimes to toil for hours with the single result of having to hold his tongue.   I used rigidly to excise the sentence, 'Nothing is known of his birth or parentage,' which tended to appear in half the lives, because where nothing is known it seems simpler that nothing should be said; and yet a man might have to consult a whole series of books before discovering even that negative fact.   The poor biographer, again, has to compress his work even at the cost of much clumsiness of style. I am painfully aware of the hideous sentences which I have constructed in trying to say in ten words what, as I fancied, might make quite a pretty passage if spread over a hundred. I have groaned over some charming anecdote which seemed to beg for a few little dramatic accessories, and wedged it remorselessly into its allotted corner, grievously perplexed by the special difficulty in our language of making the 'he's' and 'she's' refer to the proper people without the help of the detestable 'latter' and 'former.' Perhaps — so one thinks when looking at some modern biographies—the training in condensation is not altogether bad. But the problem is to condense without squeezing out the real interest. The dictionary-writer cannot dilate; but he is bound so far as he can to make the facts tell their own story. He is not to pronounce a panegyric upon heroism, but he ought so to arrange his narrative that the reader may be irresistibly led to say bravo! It is possible to make a story more pathetic by judicious reticence, though the writer who depends upon such a method needs especially appreciative readers. He must tell a good story so as to bring out the humorous side without indulging in open hilarity, though he knows painfully that many readers will not take a joke unless it is labelled 'funny,' and some will not take it till it has been hammered into their heads by repeated strokes. It follows that the ideal article should not be condensed in the sense of being reduced to the bare dates and facts capable of being arranged in mechanical order. The aim should be to give whatever would be really interesting to the most cultivated reader, though leaving it to the reader to put the dots over the i's. The writer must often make the sacrifice of keeping his most important reflection to himself; but it is not the less important that they should be in his mind. Imagine a mere antiquary and a competent student to tell within the same limits the life of some eminent philosopher or divine. The difference may be enormous between the writer who sees what are the really cardinal facts and the writer to whom any and every fact is of the same importance : and yet both narratives may appear at first sight to be equally dry and barren. I remember how a life was ridiculed by a literary critic because it explained a certain vote at the Salter's Hall Conference. The critic, who probably knew all about

Denis and Curll and the pettiest squabbles of authors, had never heard of Salter's Hall, and asked who cared for such trifles, or what it could possibly matter how anybody had voted on the occasion? Yet the conference marks a very important point in the religious history of the day, and to know how a man voted may be to define his position in a very serious controversy. The writer, that is, must give the significant facts, but has often to leave the discovery of their significance to the reader. But in order that he should appreciate their significance, he must have far wider knowledge than he can expound. The dry antiquary will often omit the vital and insert the merely accidental : he will fail to arrange them in the order or connection which makes them explain their meaning. He will resemble the witness who should fail to mention a bit of evidence which may be incidentally conclusive of a case because he is not able to appreciate its bearing. And, therefore, though the two lives might be in appearance equally dry, one may teem with useful indications to the intelligent, while the other may be as barren as it looks. The life of the divine, for example, should be given by one who has studied the theology or ecclesiastical history of the day, and who therefore knows the significance conferred upon a particular action or expression of opinion by time and place. He must abstain from exposition beyond narrow limits, and, of course, from controversy. He must not expatiate upon the bad influence of the heresy ; or attempt to show that it was a heresy. He must content himself with a pithy indication of its historical position on the development of the time ; give a sufficient summary to show how the doctrine is to be classed in its relation to the main currents of thought ; and indicate the way in which it has since been judged by competent writers, and what is the view now taken by experts. All this, which might, of course, be illustrated in other departments of biography, shows that the writer ought to be full of knowledge, which he must yet hold in reserve, or of which he must content himself with using to suggest serviceable hints. He will show incidentally why, and in what relations, certain books are worth reading or certain events worth further study ; and often, no doubt, will feel the restraint decidedly painful.

Lives well written under these conditions may, I hold, really satisfy the commemorative instinct. For the great names we shall look elsewhere : the minute names, the mere rank and file of the great army, are constantly of great use; but rather because they come into the narratives of other lives or supply data for broader histories, than because of the intrinsic interest of the story itself. But there is also an immense number of second-rate people whose lives are full of suggestion to any intelligent reader. The life in such cases should have the same kind of merit as an epitaph, though under less exacting conditions. The epitaph should give in the smallest possible number of words the very essence of a man's character and of his claims upon the memory of posterity. The life which may spread over two or three pages should aim at producing the same effect: and very frequently may give adequate expression to everything that we can really afford to remember of the less prominent actions. I will venture one illustration. There is no class of lives which has a more distinctive character than the lives of our naval heroes, from the Elizabethan days to our own. As I am not criticising the execution of the dictionary, but only indicating its main purpose, I will say nothing in praise of the particular contributor who has imbedded in its pages something like a complete naval history of the country. But

I may say this : to the mere literary reader, the ideal
of a sailor is represented by such books as Southey's
Life of Nelson ; or still more vividly perhaps by
the novels of Captain Marryat or Smollett, or by
Kingsley's *Westward Ho!* or possibly Miss Austen's
Persuasion.   We are all supposed to know something of the great admirals, upon whom R. L.
Stevenson wrote a charming article.   But any one
who is attracted by the type, would do well to turn
over the dictionary and look up the long list of
minor heroes, who stood for their portraits to
Marryat and his fellows ; the men who cut out
ships in harbour, and fought men-of-war with
merchantmen ; and lay in wait for galleons and suppressed mutinies, and had desperate single combats
with French or American frigates : the Trunnions
and Amyas Leighs and Peter Simples of real life,
who certainly are to the full as interesting as their
imaginary representatives.   Many of them have
hitherto only existed, as it were, in fragments :
their lives have to be put together from despatches
and incidental references in memoirs and histories ;
but when reconstructed, these lives form a gallery
more interesting than that at Greenwich Hospital.
They have got into a little Walhalla ; and I think
that no one will doubt who makes the experiments

either as to their deserving their places, or as to the fact that the commemoration gives a very real satisfaction to our desire to keep the memory of our worthies in tolerable repair.[1]

And, finally, this may help to justify my daring remark that the dictionary is an amusing work. This, of course, is true only upon certain conditions. The reader, as I have intimated, must supply something for himself; he has to take up the dry specimens in this great herbarium, and to expand them partly by the help of his own imagination till they take something of the form and colouring of life. Perhaps, too, it must be added, that he should know the great art of skipping, though some excellent friends of mine have told me that they read through every volume as it appears. Their state is the more gracious. Yet no man is a real reading enthusiast until he is sensible of the pleasure of turning over some miscellaneous collection, and lying like a trout in a stream snapping up, with the added charm of

[1] I am glad to see that, in this observation, I coincide with the author of *Admirals All*, who has been good enough to say a word for the dictionary in this respect. I am happy that the poetic has confirmed the prosaic judgment. Only I must add that the compliment which he pays to the editor of the dictionary is rather due to Professor Laughton, the author of the lives in question.

unsuspectedness, any of the queer little morsels of oddity or pathos that may drift past him. The old *Gentleman's Magazine* is charming in that way, but I do not know that one can find a much better hunting-ground than the dictionary. I take down a volume—honestly at random—and simply dip into it to see what will turn up. I range, as it happens, over all the centuries from Caradoc (Caractacus, the Romans called him), who fought against a Roman army backed by an elephant corps, before A.D. 50, to a gentleman of the same name, who became Lord Howden, and died in 1873 ; from Carausius, who was a bit of a pirate and something of an emperor, in the third century, and whose biographer pathetically observes that the exact dates of his life and adventures are 'not absolutely certain,' to Carlyle, in whose case the full blaze of modern biography has left not even the minutest detail untouched. There is Canute, who is not here introduced to the tide—the biographer finds out, by the way, that an anecdote is simply the polite name of a lie —and mediæval churchmen, like the admirable Chad, thanks to whom, according to Scott, the fanatic Brooke got his deserts at Lichfield, and William de St. Carilef, whose character, we regret

to say, is still puzzling, though exactly eight
hundred years have passed since he became a fair
subject for discussion. Let us hope that it will be
cleared up in time. We have that Catesby who
to most of us is known by that famous doggerel
so much more impressive than the orthodox
historical phrases about 'the cat, the rat, and
Lovel our dog,' and the other Catesby who wished
to try what would certainly have been a most
interesting philosophical experiment of blowing
King and Parliament into the air and seeing what
the country would think of it. In Tudor times
are the three Catherines who had the satisfaction of calling Henry VIII. husband, and three
Carolines to match them in the eighteenth century.
There is the Elizabethan statesman Cecil, the
great Lord Burghley, and the Robert Carr (Earl
of Somerset) who introduces us to the darkest
tragedy of the time of James I., and Lucius Cary
(Lord Falkland), who still goes about 'ingeminat-
ing peace' to remind us of the great civil war ;
and John Carteret (Earl Granville), who, in the
jovial Hanoverian days, was at the head of the
'drunken administration.' Though some of these
are sufficiently celebrated figures to be set forth in
the standard histories, they have all, I think, a

personal interest which repays a visit to them in
their homes.   At the opposite end of the scale we
have the names which, though they primarily represent mere oddities, incidentally light up odd
social phases.   Here is Margaret Catchpole, a real
heroine of romance, who stole a horse and rode
seventy miles to visit her lover, and after being
transported for an offence which excited the com-
passion of her judges, became one of the 'matri-
archs' to whom our Australian cousins trace their
descent.   There is Bampfylde Moore Carew, the
volunteer gypsy, who anticipated Borrow in the
previous generation, and gives us a passing glimpse
into the vagrant life in old English lanes and
commons.   There is John Case, astrologer, who,
as Addison tells us, made more money by his
poetry than Dryden had done in a lifetime.   It
consisted of the couplet,

> 'Within this place
> Lives Doctor Case,'

and is apparently an early triumph of the great
art of advertising.   There is the worthy Cat, who
had an 'educated and thoughtful mind,' whose
story illustrates the early growth of clubs, and
whose name has been preserved by the new style
of portraits.   There is the modern hero, Ben

Caunt, to illustrate the halo which lingered round the last days of prize-fighting. I venture to contribute a fresh anecdote to his life. I once made a pilgrimage to the place where Milton wrote the *Allegro* and *Penseroso*. The name of the poet seemed to have vanished, but a bust of the great Ben Caunt showed that the spirit of hero-worship was not extinct. Its possessor told us the story with legitimate pride. A son of the hero had brought it in a cart to an admirer after the original's death. He stopped at an inn to refresh himself 'with a bottle of soda-water,' with the result that he upset the cart at the next turning, and the bust fell upon him and killed him on the spot. The bust happily survived, and remains to kindle the enthusiasm of the villagers. Should not a Caunt be remembered as well as a Milton? He represents a type which had been characteristic, at least, of the days of the men of Trafalgar and Waterloo. A more respectable memorial of that time was the sturdy Carew (Hallowell was his name at the time) who gave to Nelson a coffin made from the mainmast of the *Orient*, to remind the great man (it was suggested) that he was still mortal. The reminder was hardly needful, one would think, just after the battle of the Nile.

Perhaps a more interesting glimpse of the same period is given by the history of Richard Carlile, the freethinker, who suffered over nine years' imprisonment for spreading opinions offensive to most of his neighbours, but of whom it is said—and, I think, justly—that he did more than any man of his time to promote the freedom of the Press. His career, at any rate, is curiously illustrative of the final struggle in that cause. If you prefer a martyrdom in a different cause, you may look at the life of Edmund Castle, who made 'an epoch in Semitic scholarship.' He was a man of property who chose to labour eighteen or nineteen hours a day at a lexicon—a dictionary-maker again ! He lost his health, suffered (it does not quite appear how) fractures and contusions of his limbs, almost lost his sight, and spent all his money. He published his immortal work by subscription, and had to wait for months at the place of sale before he could get a small part of his edition sold. The poor man got a little preferment at last towards the end of his life ; but certainly scholars will not grudge him some sympathy. I will, however, go no further. I see many more suggestive names. The Cartwrights, for example, include an important inventor of

machinery, a famous dentist, a great Puritan
divine, a Romanising bishop, the Colonel New-
come of the old reformers, and a once brilliant
dramatist.   I do not think that my dip into one
volume has produced a result differing much from
the average.   My readers must judge whether it
goes to justify my statement.   To me it seems
that at every haul one finds some specimens
which, though they require the reader to do his
part, are full of suggestions to the moderately
thoughtful reader.   'What a knowledge of human
nature you must have acquired !' has been said to
me, with a touch, I know, of sarcasm.   Perhaps
I might, if the B's had not tended to turn the A's
out of my head, and if a succinct record of a
man's main performances were the same thing as
a knowledge of the man himself.   But this I may
say ; that I have received innumerable suggestions
for thought, and had many vignettes presented to
my imagination, which to a man of any thought
or imagination should have been full of interest.
If, that is, I had been a Macaulay, I should have
approximated to that word perception of the
historical panorama which he had to construct
by assimilating the raw materials of history.
Macaulay had faults which have been so fre-

quently exposed, that the critic should perhaps be now chiefly anxious to insist upon his astonishing power in his own province. And certainly, I think that, though we should wish to see many aspects of history to which Macaulay was blind, nothing could be more delightful than to see the past as clearly, brightly, and graphically as Macaulay saw it. Nothing but a prodigious memory and a keen imagination could enable us to do that. But the dictionary well used, read thoughtfully, with the constant attempt to put flesh and blood upon the dry skeleton of facts, will, I believe, be the best help to enable any one to get as near as his faculties will permit to that desirable consummation. And, though the commemorative instinct may not be fully gratified, I think that no one can ramble through this long gallery without storing up a number of vivid images of the lesser luminaries, which will have the same effect upon his conceptions of history as a really good set of illustrations upon a narrative of travels. And, finally, I will say, what has often been a comfort to me to remember, that great as is the difference between a good and a bad work of the kind, even a very defective performance is immensely superior to none at all.

THE EVOLUTION OF EDITORS

WHAT is an editor? If we turn, as our fathers would have turned, to Johnson's *Dictionary*, we shall find in the last edition published during his life that the word in 1785 meant either ' publisher ' simply, or editor in the sense in which the name describes Bentley's relation to Horace or Warburton's to Pope. The editor, that is as implying the commander of a periodical, is not yet recognised, and Johnson, if any one, would not have overlooked him. Dr. Murray's great dictionary gives 1802 as the date of the earliest recorded use of the word in the now familiar sense. The editor is regarded by most authors as a person whose mission is the suppression of rising genius, or as a traitor who has left their ranks to help their natural enemy, the publisher. Hateful as he may be in himself, he is an interesting figure in the annals of literature. The main facts are familiar enough, and are given in various histories of the Press.[1] Yet I have found even in such books phrases which seem to imply a misconception—allusions, for example, to the 'editor and staff' of a newspaper in the days of Queen Anne. Such a slip occurs in the most perfect presentment of the spirit of that period, Thackeray's *Esmond*. Esmond goes to see the printer of *The Postboy*, and in the house encounters Swift. 'I presume you are the editor of *The Postboy*, sir?' says Swift. 'I am but a contributor,' replies Esmond. The scene is otherwise quite accurate, but Esmond, in his anxiety to be smart upon Swift, makes an anachronism. I do not know who wrote *The Postboy* at this period (1712), but it was shortly before written by Abel Boyer. Boyer was a French refugee who had to toil in Grub Street for his living. Some of his painful compilations are still known to antiquarians, and his French dictionary, or a dictionary which continued to pass under his name, survived till quite recently, if it be not still extant. He was employed by one Roper[2] to write *The Postboy*, but was turned off in 1709.

[1] I may especially refer to the last of these, Mr. Fox Bourne's *History of Newspapers*, from which I have appropriated some facts.

[2] In *Esmond*, the printer of *The Postboy* is Leach, who really printed *The Postman*. Whether Kemp, the writer mentioned by Thackeray, was a real person, I do not know.

He then published a pathetic appeal to the public, pointing out that the wicked Roper had made money by his paper, and was dismissing him without just cause. He tried, like other men in the same position, to carry on a 'true' *Postboy*, which, if ever fairly started, has vanished from the world. What kind of interviews Boyer was likely to have with Swift may be guessed from *The Journal to Stella*. Swift calls him a 'French dog who has abused me in a pamphlet'; orders a messenger to take him in charge, and requests St. John to 'swinge him.' Whoever wrote it afterwards, *The Postboy* itself was a 'tri-weekly' sheet which would go comfortably into a column of *The Times*. Its speciality, due probably to Boyer's French origin, was its foreign correspondence, and it had little else. The whole, as a rule, seems to have been made up of little paragraphs extracted from letters giving remarks about the war, and the remaining space was eked out by half a dozen advertisements. Boyer's 'editing' was all done with a pair of scissors. He was hardly more than a clerk employed by Roper to select bits of news, and probably to arrange for a supply of the necessary material.

We can make a tolerably distinct picture of the

Grub Street of this period. The street, which not long ago exchanged its ill-omened name for Milton Street, had become famous in the days of the Civil War, when the abolition of the Star Chamber gave a chance to unlicensed printers, and the appetite for news was naturally at its keenest. When order was restored it was put under restraint, and languished dismally through the Restoration period. Roger Lestrange was intrusted, not only with the superintending of the one official organ, but with power of suppressing every rival. He acted as a kind of detective, and he declares that he spent £500 a year in maintaining 'spies for information.' One night in 1663 he showed his zeal by arresting a wretched printer called Twyn. Twyn, whose only excuse was that he was the father of three poor children, was caught in the act of printing what he called 'some mettlesome stuff.' Though the stuff was too outrageous to be fully quoted even in the reports of his trial, it appears to have asserted that even kings should be responsible to their people, a doctrine which might be taken to hint at a popular rising. Twyn was sent to the gallows to clear his views of the law of libel. That law, so Scroggs declared in 1680, was that to 'publish

any newspaper whatsoever was illegal, and showed
a manifest intent to the breach of the peace.'
Although this doctrine and the practice which
it sanctioned are startling enough to us, they
suggest one significant remark.   The accounts of
Twyn's and other trials at the time prove the
infamy of Scroggs and his like, but they indirectly
prove also the advent of a change.   The reporter
had come into existence, and was doing his work
admirably.   The proceedings are taken down
word for word, and the scenes are often so vividly
described that they are more amusing, because
less long-winded, than accounts of modern trials.
Macaulay remarks that Jeffreys was awed at the
trial of the seven bishops by the 'thick rows
of earls and barons.'   The reporter contributed
equally to the remarkable change in fairness of
trials which took place at the Revolution.   It
was to be a long time before he could force his
way into the gallery of the House of Commons ;
but his influence in the law-courts was percept-
ible.[1]   The Grub Street of Boyer's time contained
many of the waifs and strays from this period of
persecution.   In wandering through that dismal

---

[1] In 1764 the reporters were liable to be turned out of court.
See XIV. *State Trials*, p. 35.

region we get the most distinct of our few
glimpses of light as from a tallow-candle held
by the crazy scribbler John Dunton.   Dunton, a
descendant of clergymen, had become a bookseller, and got into various intricate troubles, till,
as he tells us, he 'stooped so low as to become an
author,' and sank in time to be a 'willing and
everlasting drudge to the quill'! In 1705 he
published his *Life and Errors*, a book which
makes one long to ask him a few questions.   He
had seen many people of whom he could have
given interesting 'reminiscences.'   Unluckily he
did not know in what posterity would be interested.
We do not much care to know at the present day
that Richard Sault was in all probability the true
author of the *Second Spira*, a book of which
Dunton sold 30,000 copies in six weeks, and
which he now requests his readers to burn if they
meet it.   I have never had the chance of burning
it, and cannot account for his remorse, though I
hope that the sale was some consolation.   But,
besides this, Dunton had published the *Athenian
Mercury*, a sort of anticipatory *Notes and Queries*,
and to it not only this famous Sault, but John
Wesley's father and Sir William Temple and Swift
had sent contributions.   He had known, too, all

the booksellers, printers, binders, engravers, and
hackney authors of the time, and gives us tantalis-
ing glimpses of some familiar names.   He has
short descriptions of considerably over a hundred
booksellers, and from his account we are glad
to observe that they already showed their main
characteristic—the possession, namely, of all the
cardinal virtues.   He enumerates and compliments
all the writers of weekly sheets.   Among them is
Boyer, whom he praises for the 'matchless beauties
of his style'; Defoe, with whom he had unluckily
a running quarrel, and who is therefore mentioned with less warmth than inferior rivals ; and
Tutchin, whose *Observator* is 'noways inferior' to
Defoe's *Review*.   Tutchin was the famous person
who was sentenced by Jeffreys, for his share in
Monmouth's revolt, to a punishment of such
severity that he petitioned the king to be hanged
instead.   His petition is supposed to be unique,
and his prayer was not granted.   Tutchin escaped
to see Jeffreys in the Tower, and was reported
to have sent him a halter concealed in a barrel
of oysters.   Tutchin was tried in 1704 for some
of his *Observators*, in which he seems to have
obscurely hinted that there might be some corruption in the navy.   He escaped in consequence of

a technical blunder in the indictment unintelligible
to the lay reader, but, we are told, was afterwards
assaulted in consequence of some of his writings,
and so cruelly beaten that he died of his wounds.
The evidence on his trial shows clearly what a
leading newspaper was in those days.   Tutchin
had agreed with the printer to write a weekly
paper for which he was to receive 10s. 6d. a time.
The number printed was 266, and we are glad to
hear that the printer raised the price in time to 20s.
The printer incidentally admits that he had himself
done such ' editing' as was necessary ; that is, had
struck out phrases which seemed to be libellous.

Defoe and his rival Tutchin differed from
Boyer in this, that their papers were in reality
weekly pamphlets, or consisted mainly of the
matter which would now be made into leading
articles.   Tutchin and Defoe were sound Whigs,
though Defoe's Whiggism had to make awkward
compromises with his interests.   Their chief oppo-
nent was the vigorous nonjuror and voluminous
controversialist Charles Leslie, a martyr to High
Church principles, who had to live partly by his
pen, and from 1706 to 1709 published *The
Rehearsal* on the side of unflinching Jacobitism.
He escaped a trial for treason by retiring to St.

Germains. The author had always to keep one eye upon the Attorney-General, and Grub Street was a Cave of Adullam for broken men, ruined in trade or political troubles, who could just keep body and soul together by these productions. They were ' authors,' not ' editors' of their papers, and *The Review*, or *Observator*, or *Rehearsal* were simply the personal utterances of Defoe, Tutchin, and Leslie. Whether Defoe, like Tutchin, was paid by his printer, or whether, as seems more probable in so keen a man of business, he employed the printer, is more than I know. In the later years of his troublesome life, he was at one time in a position of respectability, with a comfortable house and garden, and able to provide a portion for his daughter. But Defoe was exceptional. Meanwhile the plan had been adopted in a higher sphere. Steele is distinguished in one of the lists of authors as a 'gentleman born.' The official *Gazette* had been intrusted to him with a liberal salary of £300 a year, and, as we all know, in 1709 he started *The Tatler*, which became the lineal ancestor of *The Spectator* and the long series of *British Essayists*. All the best-known authors of the eighteenth century tried their hands at this form of composition, as our grandmothers and

great-grandmothers had good cause to know.
The essays were lay sermons, whose authors condescended, it was supposed, to turn from grave
studies of philosophy or politics to topics at once
edifying and intelligible to the weaker sex. Many
of these series implied joint-stock authorship, and
therefore some kind of editing. We know, for
example, how Steele was ill-advised enough to
insert in *The Guardian* a paper by his young
admirer Pope, which ostensibly puffed their
common friend Philips's *Pastorals*, but under a
thin cover of irony contrived to compare them
very unfavourably with his own rival performances.
Pope and Philips lived afterwards, as Johnson
puts it, in a perpetual 'reciprocation of malevo-
lence'; and the editor no doubt had already
discovered that there might be thorns in his
pillow. In those happy days, too, when the
'Rev. Mr. Grove' could win immortality on the
strength of three or four papers in *The Spectator*,
Steele must no doubt have had to deal in some of
the diplomacy which is a modern editor's defence
against unwelcome volunteers. But he held no
recognised office. When he got Addison to help
him in *The Tatler*, he resembled, according to his
familiar phrase, the 'distressed prince who calls in

a powerful neighbour to his aid.' To use a humbler comparison, he was more like the preacher who asks a friend to occupy his pulpit for a Sunday or two, and finds his assistant's sermons more popular than his own. Addison and Steele appear to have started *The Spectator* in alliance, and they sold the right of publication when it was collected in a new form. The precedent was often followed by little knots of friends, and some one, of course, would have to do such editing as was wanted. One result is characteristic. There was as yet no ' We.' The writer of an essay had therefore to speak of himself in the first person ; and as the first person was not the individual writer, but the writer in his capacity as essayist, an imaginary author was invented. Hence arose the Spectator himself, and Nestor Ironside and Caleb Danvers and their like. The last representatives of the fashion were Sylvanus Urban of *The Gentleman's Magazine* and Oliver Yorke of *Fraser's*, if indeed ' Mr. Punch' is not a legitimate descendant. The fictitious author was a kind of mask to be worn by each actor in turn. But of course periodicals of this kind, which consisted of nothing but an essay supplied by some author with occasional help from his friends, required no definite editor.

Afterwards they frequently appeared as a series of articles in one of the magazines, and had less of an independent existence. For the main origin of the editor we must, then, go back to Grub Street. One point must be noticed. Between Grub Street and these higher circles of elegant authorship there was little communication, and certainly no love lost. The modern author has sometimes looked fondly back to the period of Queen Anne as a golden epoch when literature received its proper reward. Macaulay speaks of the next years as a time when the author fell, as it were, between two stools—when he had lost the patron and not been taken up by the public. This, I think, suggests an inaccurate view. Grub Street had never basked in the sunshine of patronage. Its denizens had few interviews with great men, unless they were such as Boyer had with Swift or Twyn with Lestrange. The 'hackney author,' as Dunton already calls him, was simply a nuisance to be suppressed unless he could be used as a spy. A few men of education drifted into the miserable street ; royalist divines (like Fuller) under the Commonwealth, and ejected ministers such as Baxter under Charles ii. Baxter tells us that he managed by ceaseless writing to make £70 a year, and, now and then, such men were helped by some sympathetic friend in power. But patronage, beyond an occasional bribe, or possibly a payment of hush-money, generally descended, if it descended at all, upon others than the true Grub Street author. The great men of the seventeenth century now and then acted as patrons; the two greatest English thinkers of the time, Hobbes and Locke, were supported by the Earls of Devonshire and Shaftesbury. Some patronage was bestowed upon Dryden and the poets, though they do not seem to have considered it over-liberal. Butler and Otway are the typical examples of their fate. Still, a nobleman often felt bound to send his twenty guineas in return for a dedication. Learned men, too, in the Church might of course hope for professional preferment. But all this was no comfort to the bookseller's drudge, and he got no benefits of this kind from the Revolution. What then happened was, I take it, very simple. The great man, thanks to the growth of parliamentary power, suddenly found himself enabled to be a patron at the public expense. Naturally he was suddenly seized with a fit of liberality. The famous writers of Queen Anne's

day—Addison, and Congreve, and Prior, and
their friends—became commissioners of excise, of
hackney coaches, and so forth, or found shelter in
other pleasant little offices, then newly created, of
which Ministers could dispose. Such patronage
was, of course, not given for abstruse learning ;
scholars and antiquaries were not sought out in
their studies or college lecture-rooms, or enabled
to pursue recondite researches. Still less did it
come to Grub Street. The recipients of the
golden shower were 'wits,' or men known in 'the
town,' which was no longer overshadowed by the
Court. They were selected from the agreeable
companions at one of the newly invented clubs,
where statesmen could relax over their claret and
brush up their schoolboy recollections of Horace
and Homer. Halifax, Harley, and St. John
could give a few crumbs from their table to the
men whom they met at the Kitcat or the
Brothers' Club. Swift hoped to be the founder of
an academy which should direct patronage to men
of letters, and the anecdotes of his attempts to help
his poorer brethren show the most creditable side
of his character. The pleasant time disappeared
for an obvious reason. In the reign of Queen
Anne the system of Party Government was

substantially got into working order. That meant that offices were no longer to be given away for ornamental purposes, but used for practical business. Swift called Walpole 'Bob, the poet's foe,' for his indifference to literary merit ; but Walpole was the name of a system. Places were wanted to exchange for votes, and a writer of plays and essays was not worth buying unless he were proprietor or hanger-on of the proprietor of a borough. As soon as this was clearly understood, the patronage of men of letters went out of fashion, and I greatly doubt whether literature was any the worse for the change.

Grub Street, at any rate, had been little affected by the gleam of good fortune which came to the upper circles, and was not hurt by its disappearance. The prizes bestowed upon the gentlemen and scholars who could write 'Spectator' were above the reach of Tutchin or Defoe. They had, indeed, reaped some rather questionable advantages from the political change besides the abolition of licensing. Harley was the first English statesman to use the Press systematically. Under his management the Grub Street authors ceased to be simply vermin to be hunted down ; they might be themselves used in the chase. Harley's name constantly turns up in this dismal region; he saved Boyer from Swift's wrath; he appears in the background of other obscure careers, such as that of the deist Toland; and he is specially memorable for his connection with two of the greatest of English journalists, Swift and Defoe. Swift, of course, was petted as an equal, and flattered by hopes of a bishopric; while Defoe was treated as an 'underspurleather,' a mere agent who could be handed over by Whig to Tory and Tory to Whig as the Ministry changed. Each of them, however, wrote what passed for his own individual utterance. *The Examiner*, while Swift wrote it, represented Swift, as *The Review* represented Defoe. The papers were not like modern party newspapers, complex organisms with editors and proprietors and contributors, but simply periodical pamphlets by a single author, though their utterances might be more or less inspired by the Government. The system was carried on through the Walpole period, but a change soon begins dimly to show itself. A new race is arising, called by Ralph, one of themselves, 'authors by profession,' most of whose names are familiar only to profound commentators upon the *Dunciad*. The notes to that work were, as was said, the

regular place of execution for the victims of Pope
and the blustering Warburton.   Ralph, says Warburton in one of them, 'ended in the common
sink of all such writers, a political newspaper.'
Although that represented the lowest stage of
human existence, there were some pickings to be
had even there.   The statement made by a
Committee of the House of Commons is often
quoted, that in ten years Walpole spent over
£50,000 upon the Press; over £10,000 going
to one Arnall, probably in part to be transmitted
to others.   That, as we are told, was the flourishing
period of corruption, and if authors got their
share of it their morals doubtless suffered.   And
yet we may say, if we will not be too puritanical,
that even a capacity for receiving bribes may imply
a relative improvement.   A man who can be bribed
can generally make a bargain ; he is something
more than a simple spy.   Defoe was a slave to
Ministers, who kept his conviction hanging over
his head, and just gave him scraps enough to
support him in the dirty work which he tried, very
hard it seems, but not quite successfully, to re-
concile to his conscience.   Ralph was evidently
treated with relative respect.   His moral standard
is defined by Bubb Dodington.   Ralph, says that

type of political jobbery, was 'a very honest man.' This, as Dodington's account of him shows—with no sense of incongruity—was quite compatible with a readiness to sell himself to any party. It only meant that he kept the bargain for the time. Honesty, that is, did not imply so quixotic a principle as adherence to political principles, but adherence for the time being to the man who had bought you; and even that naturally appeared an exceptionally lofty strain to Dodington. Ralph himself complains bitterly of the niggardly patronage of literature, but he ended with a pension of £600 a year. Among his allies and enemies were men like Amhurst and Arnall and Concanen and others, who, chiefly again through references in the *Dunciad*, have got their names into biographical dictionaries. Some of them gained humble rewards. Amhurst, a clever writer, who began, like Shelley, by expulsion from Oxford, seems to represent the nearest approach to the modern editor. As 'Caleb Danvers,' imaginary author of *The Craftsman*, he received the most brilliant political writing of the day from Bolingbroke, Pulteney, and the 'patriots'; and Ralph declares that he died of a broken heart when, upon Walpole's fall, his services met with no reward from his friends. *The Craftsman* was itself on *The Spectator* or *Examiner* model; but, as a party organ, inspired and partly written by the leaders of the Opposition, it had something of the position of a modern newspaper; and Amhurst, no doubt, though in a very dependent position, may be regarded as a humble forerunner of the full-blown editor of later days.

Meanwhile, however, the comparative calm of the political atmosphere under Walpole was favourable to another direction of literary development. Defoe found time for the multitudinous activities which entitle him to be a great-grand-father of all modern journalism. He helped to start newspapers; he published secret documents; he interviewed Jack Sheppard at the foot of the gallows; he collected ghost stories; he wrote accounts of worthy dissenting divines recently deceased; he wrote edifying essays upon the devil and things in general; he described tours in the country; he passed *Robinson Crusoe* through a journal like a modern *feuilleton*, and, in short, he opened almost every vein of periodical literature that has been worked by his successors. As the time goes on we find authors who really make a decent living by their pens. There is John Camp-

bell, for example, the richest author, according to
Johnson, 'who ever grazed the common of
literature'; the 'pious' gentleman on the same
authority, who, though he never entered a church,
never passed one without taking off his hat.   And
to speak of still living names, we have Richardson,
who had the good luck to be printer as well as
author, and Fielding, forced to choose between
being a hackney author or a hackney coachman,
and Johnson, who was presently to proclaim, as
Carlyle puts it, the 'blast of doom' of patronage.
The profession, or at least the trade, is beginning
to be established, and there will naturally be a
demand for editing.   The author of the loftier
sphere still laboured under the delusion that it was
unworthy of him to take money for his works.
Swift, as he tells us, never made anything, till the
judicious advice of Pope brought something for his
Miscellanies.   Pope himself, though he made his
fortune by his *Homer*, is hardly an exception.
The sums which he received, indeed, enabled him
to live at his ease, but they were the product of
a subscription, and, I fancy, of such a subscription
as has never been surpassed.   The good society of
those days held, and deserves credit for holding,
that it would do well to give a kind of national

commission to the most rising young poet of the day to produce a worthy translation of the accepted masterpiece of poetry.   It was a piece of joint-stock patronage, and not a successful publishing speculation—though it succeeded in that sense also—by which Pope made his fortune.   Grub Street, therefore, would rejoice little in a success which scarcely suggested even a precedent for imitation, and which fell to the man who was its deadliest enemy.   Pope, with his excessive sensibility, was stung by its taunts to that war with the dunces which led to his most elaborate and least creditable piece of work.   Though the bulk of his adversaries was obscure enough, the body collectively is beginning to raise its head a little. The booksellers, from Lintot to Tonson down to the disreputable Curll, are indulging in a variety of speculations from which the form of modern periodical literature begins to emerge distinctly. One symptom is remarkable.   At the beginning of 1731 the ingenious Cave, having bought a small printing - office, started *The Gentleman's Magazine*, destined to have a long life and to be followed by many imitators.   It had various obscure precursors, such as *The Historical Register*, and at first was a humble affair enough.

Most of its pages were filled with reproductions of articles from the weekly journals; but it included brief notices of books, and occasional poems and records of events and miscellaneous literature; and, in short, was complex enough to require a judicious editor. Johnson tells how Cave, when he had heard that one subscriber out of the 10,000 whom he speedily attracted was likely to drop the magazine, would say, ' Let us have something good in the next number.' Nothing more could be required to prove that Cave had the true editorial spirit. Still, however, the editor was not, and for a long time he was not to be, differentiated from the proprietor. Cave himself looked after every detail. He arranged for the parliamentary reports (a plan in which his first predecessor appears to have been our old friend Boyer in his monthly *Political State*), and employed the famous reporter who clothed the utterances of every orator of those days in sonorous Johnsonese. The success of *The Gentleman's Magazine* probably led to *The Monthly Review*, started by Ralph Griffiths in 1749, and as this was of a Whiggish turn, it was opposed by *The Critical Review*, started by Archibald Hamilton in 1756, and supported by Smollett;

a sequence like that of *The Edinburgh* and *Quarterly Reviews*. These two were the first, and till *The Edinburgh Review*, the leading representatives of literary criticism. Both of them were edited by the publishers. Griffiths, in particular, is famous as the taskmaster of Goldsmith. When a publisher has to do with a man of genius, especially with a man of genius over whom it is proper to be sentimental, he may be pretty certain of contemptuous treatment by the biographers of his client. Yet it is possible than even Griffiths had something to say for himself, and that if he was a hard master, Goldsmith may not have been a very business-like subordinate. Still, as Griffiths is said to have made £2000 a year by a venture to which Goldsmith only owed a bare escape from starvation, the printer may have been of opinion that the immediate profit was worth a good deal of posthumous abuse. However this may be, it is noticeable that the men of letters who appear in Boswell's great portrait gallery had no haven of editorship to drift into. They might be employed by the publisher of a magazine, and no doubt their drudgery would involve some of the work of a modern editor. But there was no such pillow for the wearied author as a regular

office with a fixed income and the occupation of
trimming other people's works instead of painfully
straining matter from your own brain. Good
service to a political patron, or very rarely some
other merit, might be paid by a pension ; but,
without one, even Johnson, the acknowledged
dictator of letters in his time, would apparently
have never escaped from the writer's treadmill.
He was never, it would seem, more than a month
or two ahead of the friends who have become
types of the Grub Street author : Smart, who let
himself for ninety-nine years to a bookseller, or
Boyse, whose only clothing was a blanket with
holes in it through which his hands protruded to
manufacture verses. Perhaps the Secretary of the
Literary Fund could produce parallels even at the
present day, and the increase in the prizes has
certainly not diminished the number of blanks.
Meanwhile, political journalism was coming to
fresh life with the agitation of the early days of
George III. *The North Briton*, in which Wilkes
began his warfare, was a weekly periodical
pamphlet after *The Craftsman* fashion, started
at a week's notice to meet Smollett's *Briton*,
and written chiefly by Wilkes with help from
Churchill. It had a short and stormy life, and

was not properly a newspaper.   But when Wilkes fought his later campaign, and was backed by Junius, we have at last a genuine example of a newspaper warfare of the modern kind.   *The Public Advertiser* had a significant history.   It was the new form of *The Daily Post*, started in 1719 by (or with the help of) Defoe.   The Woodfall family, well known till the end of the century, came to have the chief share in it; and in 1752 gave it a new name and form, when Fielding seems to have acted more or less as sponsor.   Upon dropping a periodical of his own, he advised his subscribers to transfer their favours to this paper, to which, moreover, he sent all his own advertisements, one as Justice of the Peace. Probably the recommendation means that it had somehow been made worth Fielding's while to let the paper have a monopoly of these notices.   It seems that fifteen years previously, the value of the paper was about £840.   By the Junius period, twenty years later, this had considerably increased. The property was held in shares, chiefly by well-known booksellers and printers.   A tenth be-longed to Henry Sampson Woodfall, who took the management from 1758, when his father died, and acted as editor for thirty-five years.   The circulation in the Junius period was about 3000 daily, and in 1774 (just after Junius had ceased) the profits were £1740. The accounts which have been preserved show the general nature of the business. The expenses, other than printing, included £200 paid to the theatres for advertisements of plays, an item which has long got to the other side of the account ; £280 for home news ; and smaller sums for foreign intelligence, and so forth. Nothing is set down for editor or contributors, and the obvious reason is that neither class existed. The contributors were some of the poor scribblers of Grub Street who collected material for paragraphs, or at times indulged in small political squibs. Contemporary portraits of the professional journalists of those days may be found in Foote's farces.[1] They are poor wretches, dependent upon 'Vamp' the bookseller, or 'Index' the printer; living in garrets, employed as hawkers of scandal, domestic and official, rising during the parliamentary session to political abuse, and in the recess picking up accounts of 'remarkable effects of thunder and lightning.' 'All is filth that comes to their net,'

---

[1] See *The Author* (1757), and *The Bankrupt* (1776).

observes one of the characters, and, in any case, they represent the class of labour which now fills up the interstices of more serious writing. *The Public Advertiser*, however, was by no means composed of such matter. If Woodfall had to pay the theatres instead of being paid by them, he got his contributors for nothing. The volunteer correspondent was apparently as abundant then as now, and the paper is chiefly filled by his lucubrations. Woodfall, who seems to have been a worthy man, prided himself especially upon his impartiality. He accepted letters from all sides, and the paper, though without leading articles, was full of lively controversy upon all the leading topics of the day ; Junius, of course, during his short career, being the most effective writer. Naturally, the paper required editing, and in a very serious sense. Woodfall was responsible when Junius assailed George III., and had to keep a very sharp eye upon the performances of his anonymous contributors. Still, however, though in point of fact an editor, he was primarily the managing partner of a business. Probably, he would receive some extra share of the profits in that capacity, and would come very near to being an editor in the

modern sense.[1]   We are told about this time that
William Dodd, the popular preacher who was
hanged for forgery in 1777, had 'descended so
low as to become editor of a newspaper'—a
degrading position which would account for a
clergyman reaching the gallows.   Still the genuine
editor has not as yet become a distinct personage.
Between this time and the revolutionary period
several of the papers were started which were to
be the main organs of public opinion down to our
own day.   On November 13th, 1776, Horace
Walpole looked out of his window and saw a body
of men marching down Piccadilly—volunteers, he
guessed, for service in the American troubles.
He was more astonished than we should be on
discovering that they were simply 'sandwich men,'
or at least men with papers in their caps or bills
in their hands, advertising a newspaper.   Henry
Bate Dudley, the 'fighting parson,' who lived to
become a baronet and a canon of Ely, was at this
time chaplain to Lord Lyttelton and employing
his leisure in writing plays, fighting duels, or
carrying on *The Morning Post*.   It had begun
four years earlier, and Bate was now appealing for

[1] A ledger of *The Public Advertiser*, from 1766 to 1771, is now in
the Free Library at Chelsea, to which it was presented by Sir C. Dilke.

support against a rival who was starting a new
Morning Post.   Bate, as Walpole says, is 'author'
(still not editor) of the old *Morning Post;* and in
1780 he left it to set up *The Morning Herald* in
opposition.   A duel or two and a confinement for
a year in the King's Bench prison varied his
amusements.   Walpole moralises after his fashion
upon the 'expensive masquerade exhibited by a
clergyman in defence of daily scandal against
women of the highest rank, in the midst of a civil
war'!   I do not know how far *The Morning Post*
deserved this imputation ; but its history shortly
afterwards brings us within reach of the modern
system.   Three men in particular played a great
part in the transformation of the newspaper ; two
of them, as might be anticipated, were energetic
young Scots, and one of these came from Aberdeen,
the centre, as many of its inhabitants have told
me, whence spread all good things.   Perry, Stuart,
and Walter were these creators of the modern
newspaper, and their history shows how the 'able
editor' finally came to life.   The first Walter
was a bookseller, who thought that he could turn
to account an invention called 'logography' (the
types were to be whole words instead of letters)
by printing a newspaper.   Though the invention

failed, the newspaper lived for a short time as *The Universal Register*, and became *The Times* on January 1, 1788. Walter's first declarations show how accurately he had devised the conditions of success. His ideal paper was to give something for all tastes; it was not to be merely commercial nor merely political, it was to represent public opinion generally, not any particular party, and it was never 'to offend the ear of delicacy.' When it had survived logography and obtained its incomparable monosyllabic name, it was fitted for a successful career. The war was an ill wind enough, but it blew prosperity to newspapers as the wars of the Great Rebellion and of Queen Anne's day had given fresh impulse to its infancy and boyhood. Walter, too, and his son, who took the helm in 1802, were keen in applying mechanical improvements and organising the new machinery. *The Times* seems to have invented the foreign correspondent, its representative, Henry Crabb Robinson, being probably the first specimen of the genus : it beat the Government in getting the first news of battles, and defeated a strike of the printers in order to introduce a new method of printing. The younger Walter, however, seems still to have combined the functions of editor and proprietor until 1810, when Sir John Stoddart became editor.   Stoddart was succeeded by Barnes in 1817, and Barnes in 1841 by Delane, when editorship had become not only a separate function, but a position of high political importance.   James Perry, meanwhile, had come into the profession from a different side.   He had been early thrown upon his own resources, and about 1777 sent some articles to a newspaper which gained him employment at the rate of a guinea and a half a week.   He soon rose to a better position.   *The Morning Chronicle* had been started in 1769 by William Woodfall (younger brother of Henry Sampson), who gained the nickname 'Memory Woodfall' from his powers of bringing back debates in his head.   His reports became the great feature of *The Chronicle* ; but Perry, who was getting four guineas a week for editing *The Gazetteer*, succeeded in beating Woodfall by employing a staff of reporters.   *The Chronicle* began to decline.   Perry, managing with the help of a friend to scrape together about £1000, bought the paper and made it the accepted organ of the Whig Party.   It soon became a leading paper, and was for a time at the head of the London Press.   It was ultimately sold after

Perry's death in 1821 for £42,000. Perry
appears to have edited it himself until 1817, when
his mantle fell upon another vigorous Scot, John
Black, who had joined it as a reporter. Black
and Barnes thus started simultaneously, Black
representing the opinions of the 'philosophical
Radicals,' and being steadily inspired by James
Mill. Thus Perry, like Walter, marks the end of
the period in which the proprietor still habitually
acted as editor.

Perry at various times received contributions
from many of the most eminent writers of the
time. Coleridge got a guinea out of him at a
critical moment. Thomas Campbell published
Ye Mariners of England in *The Chronicle*
Charles Lamb sent him paragraphs ; Sheridan,
Mackintosh, Hazlitt, Tom Moore were among his
contributors ; and Lord Campbell, better known
as The Chancellor, was for a time both law
reporter and theatrical critic. The last of the
three rulers of the Press, Daniel Stuart, is still
often mentioned for a similar reason. Stuart, like
Perry, a vigorous Scot, had joined his brothers,
who were settled as printers in London. They
printed *The Morning Post*, which had fallen into
difficulties ; and in 1795, when its circulation was

only 350 copies daily, Daniel Stuart bought the
paper, land, and plant for £600. He raised
the circulation to 4500 in 1803, when it was
surpassed in popularity by *The Chronicle* alone.
He soon afterwards became the owner of *The
Courier* in partnership with one Street, gave up
The Post, and in 1822 retired, having made a
fortune.   Stuart was specially connected with
Mackintosh, who married his sister when they were
both struggling young men.   His fame, however,
rests more upon his connection with Coleridge,
and he incurred the danger which comes to all
publishers of works of men of genius.   Certain
phrases in Coleridge's *Biographia Libraria* and
Table Talk gave rise to the impression that Stuart
was one of the conventional bloodsuckers, who
make their money out of rising genius and repay
them with the scantiest pittance.   Stuart defended
himself effectively ; and any doubts which might
remain have been dispersed by the (privately
printed) *Letters from the Lake Poets*.   Stuart, in
fact, was one of the most helpful of Coleridge's
many friends, and Coleridge to the end of his
life spoke of him and to him with warm and
generous gratitude.   Coleridge, it is clear enough,
and certainly very natural, took at times an

exaggerated view of his services to *The Morning Chronicle.* His surprising statement that Stuart in 1800 offered him £2000 a year if he would devote himself to journalism, that he declined on the ground that he would not give up 'the reading of old folios' for twenty times £2000, and that he considered any pay beyond £350 as a real evil, is obviously impossible. Stuart had probably tried to spur his indolent contributor by saying that his services would be worth some such sum if they could be made regular. But the statement is only worth notice here in illustration of the state of the literary market at the time. Southey acknowledges his gratitude for the guinea a week which he received as Stuart's 'laureate.' Poetry, by the way, appears to have been more in demand then than at the present day. Both Perry and Stuart's elder brother offered to employ Burns ; and Coleridge, Southey, Campbell, and Moore all published poems in the newspapers. Lamb tried his hand at 'jokes.' 'Sixpence a joke,' he says, 'and it was thought pretty high, too, was Dan Stuart's settled remuneration in these cases' (*Newspapers Thirty-five Years Ago*), and no paragraph was to exceed seven lines. In a letter of 1803, Lamb says that he has given up his 'two guineas a week' from *The Post.* The high-water mark of a journalist's earnings at the end of the last century is probably marked by the achievement of Mackintosh, who earned ten guineas in a week. 'No paper could stand it!' exclaimed the proprietor, and the bargain had to be revised. A few years later, however, we are told that Sterling, the father of Carlyle's friend, was receiving the sum which Coleridge supposed himself to have refused, namely, £2000 a year for writing leading articles in *The Times.* Stuart, it would seem, in the earlier period was paying the fair value of their wares to Coleridge, Southey, and their like; but in the days of Scott and Byron the price of popular writing was going up by leaps and bounds.

The normal process of the evolution of editors was what I have tried to sketch, simply, that is, the gradual delegation of powers by the printer or bookseller who had first employed some inhabitant of Grub Street as a drudge, and when the work became too complex and delicate, had handed over the duties to men of special literary training. Two very important periodicals, however, of this period show a certain reversion to the older type. *The Edinburgh Review* owed part of its success to its independence of publishers. It was started, not by a speculator who might wish to puff his own wares, but by a little knot of audacious youths, who combined as Steele and Addison combined in *The Spectator*. It seems that at first they scarcely even contemplated the necessity of an editor, and Sydney Smith was less editor than president of the little committee of authors at the start. When Jeffrey took up the duty, he was careful to make it understood that his work was to be strictly subordinate to his professional labours, and had no inkling that his fame would come to depend upon his editorship. *The Edinburgh*, however, soon became a review of the normal kind. Cobbett, on the other hand, started his *Political Register* as a kind of rival to *The Annual Register*. It was to be mainly a collection of State papers and official documents ; but it soon changed in his hands into the likeness of Defoe's old *Review*. It became a personal manifesto of Cobbett himself, and, as such, held a most important place in the journalism of the time. But Cobbett was, and in some ways remains, unique, and, as the newspaper has developed, the 'we' has superseded the 'I,' and the organism become too complex to represent any single person. The history, indeed, would help to explain various peculiarities characteristic of English newspapers, especially the bad odour which long adhered to the profession, and made even Warrington ashamed to confess to Pendennis that he was a contributor to a leading newspaper. The author by profession of the time of Ralph had excellent reasons for concealing his name, and the desire for anonymity long survived the old justification. But I have said enough to leave that and other considerations untouched for the present.

JOHN BYROM

Who was John Byrom? That is a question to which, if it were set in an examination for students of English literature, an answer might reasonably be expected, but which, if put to less omniscient persons, might not improbably receive a rather vague reply. And yet an answer might be given which would awake some familiar associations. John Byrom was the author of two or three epigrams which for some reason have retained their vitality well into a second century of existence. The unmusical are still happy to recall the comparison between Handel and Buononcini, and to wonder that there should be such a difference between 'tweedle-dum and tweedle-dee,' though they are apt to assign to Swift instead of Byrom the credit of being the first worm to turn against the contempt of more happily endowed natures. There is the still more familiar verse, ending :—

> But who Pretender is, and who is King,
> God bless us all, that's quite another thing.

And there is a certain assault upon ' Bone and Skin, two millers thin,' which—though the real names of the millers and the circumstances which induced the declaration that flesh and blood could not bear them have long vanished out of all but antiquarian memories—have somehow continued to go on jingling in men's ears ever since 17th December 1728. I have said enough to suggest more than one problem. What is the salt which has kept these fragments of rhyme so long alive? Is it due to the sound or the sense? Survival for a century has been given as the test which entitles a man to be called a classic. Does the survival of these little impromptus entitle Byrom to be a classic? May we call them jewels five lines long, that are to sparkle for ever on the stretched fore-finger of all time? That seems to be too lofty a claim. The thought is not by itself very subtle or very keen. And yet when we think how few are the writers who can blow even the frailest of word-bubbles which shall go floating down five or six generations, we must admit the fact to be remarkable. What is the quality which it indicates in the author? And here I might affect to take up the psychological method : show what are the peculiarities necessarily implied by success in these little achievements ; deduce from them what must have been the characteristics of Byrom's mind and temperament; and finally, by appealing to facts, show how strikingly the *à priori* reasoning would be confirmed by experience. I think that a little ingenuity might enable an ambitious critic to give plausibility to such a procedure; but I prefer to take a humbler method, for which sufficient materials have been lately provided. Byrom, I may remark, in the first place, is hardly thought, even by his warm admirers, to be other than a second-rate poet : nor need I appeal to the Latin grammar to prove that second-rate poetry is not generally worth reading. The reason is, I suppose, that a second-rate poet only does badly what has been done well, whereas even a tenth-rate historian or philosopher may be giving something new. That reason, at least, will do sufficiently well to suggest why an exception may be made in favour of some second-rate poetry. There are cases in which poetry not of the highest class reveals a charm of character peculiar to itself, though not of the highest kind. We cannot help loving the writer, though we admit that he was not a Dante, or a Shakespeare, nor even—in this case the comparison is more to the purpose—

a Pope. The first condition of this kind of charm is, of course, perfect simplicity. The poet must be really showing us his heart, not getting upon stilts and trying to pour out epic poems and Pindaric odes, after the fashion of some of Byrom's contemporaries. Glover's *Leonidas* and Mason's odes have long been swept into the limbo where such things go; but the excellent Byrom, who is content to be himself, and whose self happened to be a very attractive one, may be still read with pleasure. Indeed, and this is what prompts me to speak of him just now, he has found an editor who reads him with enthusiasm as well as pleasure. Four handsome volumes[1] have recently been published by the Chetham Society under the care of Dr. Ward, Principal of the Owens College. Dr. Ward has done his work in the most loving spirit; he has pointed out with affectionate solicitude everything that strikes him as admirable in Byrom's poetry; he has not been so blinded by zeal as to try to force upon us admiration for the weaker pieces at the point of the critical bayonet; and he has given with overflowing learning everything that a reader can possibly require for the due apprecia-

---

[1] Two volumes, each in two parts, properly.

tion of incidental circumstances.   I fear that I am
not quite a worthy follower; my admiration of
Byrom's poetry stops a little further this side of
idolatry; and, therefore, I frankly admit that Dr.
Ward is likely to be a better guide than I to
those who are accessible to Byrom's charm.   In
such cases excess of zeal is far less blamable than
defect.   Still, I hope that in a liking for Byrom
himself I am not altogether unworthy to follow
in his admirer's steps; and it is of the man himself that I propose chiefly to speak.   Byrom, as
I think, is a very attractive example of a charming
type of humanity; and shows qualities really
characteristic of the period, though too often overlooked in our popular summaries.   He flourished
during the literary reigns of Addison and Pope;
and the splendour of their fame is too often
allowed to blind us to the peculiarities of some of
the secondary luminaries.

Byrom has already been made known to us by
his 'remains,' published for the Chetham Society
some forty years ago.   Of this, Dr. Ward says
that, were it more widely known, it would be 'one
of the most popular works of English biographical literature.'   It is, I think, only fair to warn
any one who is tempted to rush at once to a

library to procure this fascinating work, that it will not yield up its charm—a charm there certainly is—without a certain amount of perseverance. A good deal of it is a skeleton diary—mere statements of small facts, which, if interesting at all, are interesting only when you have enabled yourself to read a good deal between the actually written lines—and, moreover, Byrom is apt to be t ntalising, and to confine himself to brief notes just where we should be glad of a little more expansion. He meets Laurence Sterne, for example, and repeats not a word of his talk. After making this reservation, I can fully agree with Dr. Ward, that it is impossible to read through the book without deriving a charming impression of Byrom himself, and of the circle in which he especially delighted.

And now I will try to answer briefly the question from which I started. Who was Byrom? Byrom was the descendant of an old family long settled near Manchester. The Byroms of Byrom had dwindled down till they were represented by one Beau Byrom, who, in the time of his cousin, was consuming the last fragments of the ancestral estates, was subsiding into a debtor's prison, and was not above accepting a half-crown

from his more prosperous relative. The Byroms
of Manchester were meanwhile prospering in
business. Manchester was then a country town
of some 30,000 inhabitants, beginning to take a
certain interest in a Bill permitting a freer use
of cotton ; but not, as yet, feeling itself aggrieved
by exclusion from a Parliamentary representation.
The upper classes had a strong tincture of the
Jacobitism prevalent in the Lancashire of those
days ; and John, born in 1692, was clearly
brought up in this faith. He was sent to Trinity
College, Cambridge, then under the rule of the
great Bentley, who was at the time beginning the
famous legal warfare which was to display his
boundless pugnacity and fertility of resource in
litigation. Nobody was less inclined to sympathise with excessive quarrelsomeness than Byrom ;
but the young man, who became scholar and
fellow of his college, was always on most friendly
terms with the master. Bentley could be good
company when his antipathies were not aroused ;
and Byrom was welcomed to the great man's
domestic circle. Incidentally this led to the performance which made him in a modest way
famous for years to come. *The Spectator* had
been revived in 1714, when Byrom was about

to gain his fellowship. The young man sent to
it a couple of papers which were published in the
famous journal—a success sufficient to give him
a kind of patent of authorship. He followed it
up by the more successful 'pastoral,' addressed to
Phebe. Phebe was Joanna or 'Jug' Bentley, the
master's youngest daughter. She was destined to
be the mother of the Cumberland described by
Goldsmith as 'The Terence of England, the
mender of hearts,' but perhaps better known as
Sheridan's *Sir Fretful Plagiary*. She was, as her
son intimates, a witty young lady, sometimes coy
and silent, and sometimes a little too smart in her
satire. More than one of the college fellows
were fascinated by her in later days, and even
brought to take her father's side in his disputes.
One of the superseded laments[1] her

> haughtiness of mien,
> And all the father in the daughter seen.

At this period, though she was only eleven, she
probably showed symptoms enough of these
characteristics to suggest the tone of Byrom's
famous verses. Famous they certainly were in his
day, for his friends constantly ask him for copies ;

[1] See his poem in Nichol's *Literary Anecdotes*, i. 244.

but perhaps they are not so famous now as to
forbid a specimen.   Colin is terribly put out by
Phebe's absence.

> My dog I was ever well pleaséd to see
> Come wagging his tail to my fair one and me :
> And Phebe was pleased too, and to my dog said,
> 'Come hither, poor fellow,' and patted his head.
> But now, when he 's fawning, I with a sour look
> Cry 'Sirrah,' and give him a blow with my crook ;
> And I 'll give him another ; for why should not Tray
> Be as dull as his master when Phebe 's away ?

'I 'll give him another' is a phrase for which I
have often been grateful to the excellent Byrom.
It gives a pleasant sanction to one's own humours.
Though the metre limps a little in this stanza, it
is often very dexterously used by Byrom ; and the
poem is worthy of a high place in the age of
Mat Prior.   Probably, though an absurd con-
struction has been put upon the facts, the master
was not the less friendly towards the young fellow
for this compliment to his bright little daughter.
' Mr. Spectator' judged rightly that it would divert
his readers ; and a Mr. Mills, years afterwards,
' kissed the book ' when he read it.

Byrom had some difficulty at the time in taking
the oaths to the new family ; and he made a rather
mysterious journey soon afterwards to Montpellier.

He professed to be studying medicine, and was afterwards often called 'doctor.' It was, however, strongly suspected that his journey had a political purpose. He certainly kissed the Pretender's hand at Avignon. He returned after a time to Manchester, where, in 1721, he married his cousin, Elizabeth Byrom. His father was dead; and the family property had gone to his elder brother. Byrom was therefore in want of money, and the measure which he took for obtaining supplies was characteristic, and led him into a peculiar career. Byrom would not have been the man he was without a hobby. In fact, he so far shared the spirit of the Shandy family that he had a whole stable of hobbies. He belongs on one side to the species which has been celebrated by so many of the eighteenth-century humorists. He would have appreciated Sir Roger de Coverley, or Parson Adams, or Uncle Toby, or the Vicar of Wakefield. The kindly simplicity which takes a different colouring in each of those friends of our imagination was fully realised in Byrom. He was evidently overflowing with the milk of human kindness; attaching himself to every variety of person, from the great Bentley to the burlesque Sam Johnson, author of *Hurlothrumbo*; appreciating

them as cordially as Boswell, and alienated by
nothing but censorious harshness.   But, through
all, he has a quaint turn of mind which shows
alternately the two aspects of genuine humour—a
perception of the absurd side of other people's
crotchets, or an addiction to some pet crotchet
of his own.   Now the great discovery upon which
he prided himself was a system of shorthand.   He
had, it seems, invented a system in combination
with a friend at college; and he now bethought
himself of turning this invention to account.
Shorthand was by no means a novelty; and we all
remember how Pepys had employed the invention;
but Byrom's was, so he believed, the very perfection of shorthand—'Beauty, Brevity, and
Perspicuity' were, he says, its characteristics.   He
set about propagating the true faith with infinite
zeal.   In London he found a rival, one Weston,
who was making a living by giving lessons in the
art.   Weston challenged him to display his skill,
and put bragging advertisements in the papers to
claim superiority.   Byrom felt that his dignity
might be compromised by a contest with a
commonplace teacher.   His own shorthand was
founded on scientific principles, and was a mystery
to be imparted to the nobility and gentry; whereas

Weston was a mere empiric, and, moreover, a vulgar person who talked broad Scotch. Byrom, therefore, retorted only by some humorous remarks, and apparently made peace with his humble rival. He served as umpire at a contest between Weston and another pretender to the art, and laid down the law with the lofty superiority of a fellow of the Royal Society. When invited to take notes at a famous law-case in those days he doubts his own ability and even recommends a trial of Weston. His own shorthand was too good, he seems to imply, to be exposed to the vulgar test of mere speed of writing. Experts, in fact, say that its defects in this respect led to its being superseded in the next generation. Meanwhile, however, Byrom not only believed himself, but collected a body of believers. They formed a shorthand society; they had periodical meetings, and addressed each other as ' brothers in shorthand.' Byrom was greeted as Grand Master, and pronounced a solemn oration at their first gathering. Its preparation during two or three previous weeks is noted in his journal. He takes the highest possible tone. He humorously traces back his art to the remotest antiquity; he intimates that Plato probably used shorthand to take down the conversation of Socrates, and finds shorthand even in Egyptian hieroglyphics. The divine Tully, however, is his great model, and he shows by an ingenious emendation (*notare* for *natare*) that the Emperor Augustus taught his nephews, not to swim, but to take notes. He points out that amidst all the vices of Caligula, one which was thought to deserve notice was his ignorance of shorthand. Making a rapid bound over the intervening period, with one brief touch at the Abbot Trithemius, he appeals to the patriotism of his hearers to support what was at this time held to be a specially English art. A formal paper is drawn up, beginning, *Quod felix faustumque sit*, and declaring that the signers will form a society, *ad tachygraphiam nostram ediscendam, promovendam, et perpetuandam, in secula seculorum, Amen.*

The meetings of the shorthanders naturally took place at taverns, and they formed a kind of club after the fashion of the day. Byrom took five guineas from each aspirant to the art, and a promise not to divulge the secret. They had apparently very pleasant meetings, and diverged from shorthand into discussions of politics, theology, free-will, and things in general. On one

occasion, for example, when Byrom observes that
he was in ' a talking humour,' which was certainly
not rare, he discusses the Babylonian and Coptic
letters, the probabilities of the devil being saved,
and ' Dr. Dens' drawer of daggers.' Unluckily,
the remarks which threw light upon these topics
are not reported. The society seems to have done
its duty in loyally spreading its president's fame.
Great men became his pupils. The most famous
in early years was Lord Chesterfield ; Horace
Walpole afterwards took some lessons. His
warmest friend was the amiable philosopher,
David Hartley, who cordially supported him
in efforts to raise a subscription for a publication of his method once for all. Although this
came to nothing, Byrom, in 1742, obtained
an Act of Parliament which gave him the
right of publishing and teaching for twenty-one
years.

It was while he was engaged upon this pro-
paganda that most of the diary was written.
Manchester, of course, did not afford aspirants
enough to maintain a teacher. Byrom had,
therefore, to leave his family and pass months
together in London and at Cambridge, where he had
kept up many friendships. Travelling, of course,

was a serious business.   He generally makes two days of the fifty miles from London to Cambridge, though he once does it without an upset in less than nine hours.   Now and then there is mention of a coach, but he is generally on horseback. Sometimes he rides post on 'little hobbling horses,' which leave him with aching arms after forty or fifty miles.   Oftener it seems that he buys a horse at Manchester for five pounds or so, and sells it when he gets to London, and his horses are apt to turn out blind or lame.   Once he collects a party of half a dozen friends and makes a walking tour from London, through Oxford, Worcester, and Shrewsbury to Manchester.   It is to be regretted that he scarcely gives more than glimpses of these little tours.   They suggest dimly the days when the wanderer had to plunge through labyrinths of muddy lanes ; when he had to take a guide from one halting-place to another, and make inquiries of knowing persons as to the proper turning where you should leave the great northern road to diverge to Manchester.   I see no indications, either here or in the poems, that the excellent Byrom cared for 'nature' in the shape of scenery.   He had none of the love for field-sports which in those days might serve as an excuse for enjoying the country. ' Nay,' he observes, when some one sends him a hare,

> Nay, should one reflect upon cruelty's course,
> In the gentlemen butchers, the Hunt, and the Course,
> 'Twere enough to prevent either pudding or jelly
> From storing such carcass within a man's belly !

Here and there he has an adventure. He has a gift for falling in with the most deserving beggars, poor soldiers who have been 'in slavery' some-where, and the like, and gives them money and letters to his friends. Once, in Epping Forest, on the way to Cambridge, he has the proper meeting with a highwayman. Of course, he takes it good-humouredly, as an excellent pretext for a copy of verses. The highwayman's bad language runs spontaneously into rhyme ; and in proper epical style the ruffian is put to flight by the mock-heroic vision of the ' Goddess Shorthand, bright, celestial maid ' ! In sober prose, the highwayman goes off with a guinea of Byrom's, and Byrom expects to see him again in the neighbourhood of Tyburn. Byrom, however, is really happy when he is in the full stream of society. One of his friends describes a typical London day from imagination, which, as the diary shows, is very nearly correct. He generally gets up late, we are sorry to observe,

but he has often been sitting up at a club, or sometimes studying Hebrew till two or three in the
morning.   He has a meagre dish of tea, reads the
equally meagre papers, and groans over his absence
from Mrs. Byrom and his family.   Then he turns
out to give a lesson in shorthand.   He is tempted
to 'a hedge-booksellers in some bye-lane.'   He is
in the habit of denouncing the love of book-buying
as a vanity, but he cannot resist it.   He buys some
queer old volume—mystical divinity if possible—
and, to do him justice, seldom gets to a pound and
often descends to fourpence.   Afterwards he drops
in upon friendly Dr. Hartley and his charming
wife, and discusses the chances of a subscription for
his book.   He fills up time by an interview with
a member of some eccentric sect ; and, finally,
meets a knot of friends at a tavern.   Byrom, of
course, was strictly temperate, though he seems to
have tried his digestion by some rather odd
mixtures (such as cream and ale), and equally of
course, he is, though not quite systematically, a
vegetarian.   He would have been an anti-vaccina-
tionist, and already denounces inoculation.   His
friends dearly like to pay him little compliments
by asking for a copy of 'My time, O ye Muses,'
or his epigram on Handel and Buononcini.   Now

and then he extemporises a copy of verses on the appearance of the president of a club, for example, in ' a black bob-wig.' What can be the cause ?

A phrenzy ? or a periwigmanee
That overruns his pericranie ?

That he could enjoy some amusements which seem scarcely in character is proved by the verses on Figg and Sutton, done into prose in Thackeray's *Virginians*, and Dr. Ward has to remind us that this was ' not a brutal prize-fight,' but an ultra-vigorous ' assault-at-arms.' The line seems rather hard to draw. Byrom at least sympathises with the familiar sentiment about the ' British Grenadier.'

Were Hector himself, with Apollo to back him,
To encounter with Sutton,—zooks! how he would thwack
    him!
Or Achilles, though old Mother Thetis had dipt him,
With Figg—odds my life! how he would have unript him!

Another of Byrom's characteristic performances was prompted by his interest in his fellow-townsman, Samuel Johnson, a fiddler and dancing-master, who produced a strange medley called *Hurlothrumbo*. Dr. Ward, who has read it, as in duty bound, says that it is sheer burlesque, though some critics seem to be haunted by an uncomfortable suspicion that its apparent madness conceals some sparks of genius.   Anyhow, Byrom took it as farce, and, partly for the fun of the thing, and partly from a good-natured wish to be of use to the author, contributed an amusing epilogue and attended the first performance in London.   There were seven or eight 'garters' in the pit ; Byrom led the *claque*.   The audience took the joke.   The play ran for thirty nights ; the name got a place in popular slang, and Johnson appears to have been grateful, whether he quite perceived or not that Byrom was laughing in his sleeve.   'For my part,' says Byrom to his wife, 'who think all stage entertainments stuff and nonsense, I consider this as a joke upon 'em all.'

This, indeed, marks Byrom's peculiar vein. Hitherto I have spoken of him as an admirably good-natured humorist and lover of harmless fun. He can go to a tavern or Figg's 'amphitheatre,' and, to all appearance, throw himself into the spirit of the performances as heartily as any of his companions.   Yet, at the same time, he was a man of very deep and peculiar religious sentiments. In this matter of the play, he gradually came, it seems, to take a stricter view.   The denunciation of the stage by the nonjuror Jeremy Collier had become famous.   Arthur Bedford, an orthodox clergyman, had (in 1719) collected 7000 'immoral sentiments from British dramatists' to prove the same point, and William Law, Byrom's great teacher, had demonstrated in a treatise the absolute unlawfulness of stage entertainments (1726), and had elsewhere declared that 'the playhouse was as certainly the house of the devil as the church was the house of God.' Byrom was, perhaps, one of those people who could not be too hard even upon the 'puir de'il.' He was, at least, willing to try the effect of good-humoured raillery on the evil one before proceeding to stronger measures. When one of his friends complains of Law's severity in this matter, Byrom is evidently puzzled. His reverence for Law struggles with a sense that the oracle was rather harsh. But in other matters Byrom's loyalty was boundless. Byrom's interest in various representatives of the religious speculations of the time is shown constantly in his diaries. He meets William Whiston, the successor to Newton's professorship, who had been deprived of his place as a heretic, and went about in all societies (he appears in the well-known picture of Tunbridge Wells with Richardson, Chesterfield, and the rest) trying to propagate what he took to be primitive

Christianity. Dr. Primrose, as we know, was unlucky enough to be converted to his doctrine of monogamy. In simplicity and honesty he was worthy to make friends with Byrom; but, to say the truth, he appears in the diary rather in the character of a conceited bore. He had not Byrom's saving sense of humour. Then there was Edward Elwall, who was tried for blasphemy because he taught the 'perpetual obligation' of the Jewish law, and consequently wore a beard and a Turkish habit (the 'habit' out of respect, we are told, for the Mohammedans), and shut his shop on Saturdays. King George, he said, according to Dr. Johnson, if he were afraid to dispute with a poor old man, might bring a thousand of his blackguards with him; and, if that would not do, a thousand of his red guards. He seems, however, to have got out of his troubles, and was duly interviewed by Byrom. Byrom met more remarkable personages. He knew something of the Wesleys, and he had one of the few recorded interviews with Bishop Butler. They had a long discussion as to the claims of reason and authority. The bishop, one may guess, got rather the best of it, as Byrom admits that he was himself too warm, while the bishop was conspicuously mild

and candid. Unluckily, Byrom was an inadequate
Boswell, and is so anxious to record his own
argument on behalf of authority that he does not
quite let us know what Butler had to say for
reason. Law, however, is by far the most conspicuous figure. Law, when Byrom first went to
see him (4th March 1729), was living in the
house of old Mr. Gibbon at Putney, and acting
as tutor to the younger Gibbon, afterwards father
of the historian. He had been at Cambridge in
Byrom's time, had got into difficulties for his
Jacobite proclivities, and, by refusing to take the
oaths, had cut himself off from an active clerical
career. Byrom would sympathise with him upon
this ground; but it was the recently published
Serious Call which led to the new connection.
Byrom bought the book in February 1729, and
at once felt the influence, which made its perusal
a turning-point in the lives of many eminent men
of the day. To him it was especially congenial.
Law afterwards became a disciple of Jacob Böhme,
and Byrom, though he accepted the later utterances with reverence, confessed that they were
above his comprehension. Of such matters, I may
say that at a later period Law might probably
have been, like Coleridge, a follower of Schelling,

and have clothed his thought in the language of transcendental metaphysics rather than of the old theosophy. He was no mere dreamer or word-maker. If to his contemporaries he seemed to be talking mere jargon, later critics have thought that his position showed a real insight into the intel-lectual deficiencies of the time. But, in any case, he was, as Gibbon declares, ' a wit and a scholar ' ; had not his mind been ' clouded with enthusiasm ' he would have been one of the most agreeable authors of the day ; and his portraits in the *Serious Call* are ' not unworthy of the pen of La Bruyère.' These compliments from Gibbon are significant. Neither Law nor Byrom were con-temporaries of Addison and Pope for nothing. However far they were from the ordinary tone of religion and philosophy, they could both mix in the society of the day, and write as brightly and observe as keenly as the ordinary frequenter of clubs and coffee-houses. Their mysticism was not mere muddle. They show that a man may have the sparkle and clearness of the wits of Queen Anne allied with a steady flow of sweet and tender sentiment.

Byrom had already shown his fitness to be a disciple of Law. One of his pleasantest copies of verses tells how, in 1727, he bought a picture of Malebranche, a philosopher naturally revered by both. Byrom describes his eagerness in going to the auction, his palpitations when the portrait of the great teacher was brought out, the haste with which he advanced his biddings, and how he gets the picture for three pounds five shillings. His ecstasy is indescribable! Let your duchesses throw away ten times as many guineas on pictures of nobodies by famous artists. Byrom has got his Malebranche, 'the greatest divine that e'er lived upon earth,' whips into a coach, calls to the driver to go as fast as he can spin; deposits the treasure at his chambers, and summons his friend to come and rejoice; let him bring a friend or two to 'mix metaphysics, and shorthand, and port.' What, he exclaims, can 'be more clever'?

Huzza! Father Malebranche, and Shorthand for ever!

The *Serious Call* inspired another poem. When Byrom, a few days after reading it, made his first call upon the author, he had in his pocket a versification of a quaint parable which it contains. Law compares the man whose heart is set upon the world to a person with a monomania about a pond. He passes his life in trying to keep the pond full, and is finally drowned in it.   This struck Byrom's fancy.   He expands it into a fable in verse, and ventures to show his performance to Law himself.   Law laughed, and begged him not to turn the whole book into verse, 'for then it would not sell in prose—so the good man can joke.'   This was before the rise of the Authors' Society, and the value of a copyright was still a subject for 'joking.'   In later days Law encouraged Byrom to versify other works, and seems to have thought that the effect would be to advertise the prose.   He calls Byrom his laureate ; but Byrom, I suspect, did not contribute much to Law's popularity.   The poems had not a large circulation.

Some of his other religious poems have great merits.   Of an early paraphrase of the 23rd Psalm I will only say that Dr. Ward endorses the statement of a Mr. Hedges, that he 'would give all the world to have been able to have done them.' It is in the same metre as the pastoral, and like that poem owes its charm to the entire simplicity which enables Byrom as a reverential interpreter to catch the charm of that masterpiece of Hebrew poetry.   Another poem,

> Christians, awake! salute the happy morn,
> Whereon the Saviour of the world was born,

has been often reprinted, and is given in *Hymns Ancient and Modern*. I may infer that it is at least as familiar to my readers as to myself. It probably marks Byrom's highest level, though some other of his religious poems, especially those in which he celebrates his favourite virtue, contentment, have the same charm. They breathe, at least, the sweetness and simplicity of the writer's own character. I will quote one little fragment as at once brief and characteristic :—

> O happy Resignation!
>   That rises by its fall!
> That seeks no exaltation,
>   But wins by losing all;
> That conquers by complying,
>   Triumphing in its lot;
> That lives when it's a-dying,
>   And is when it is not!

The longer pieces, in which Byrom versified Law's works with more or less closeness, come nearer to the conventional style of the period, and drop pretty frequently into the flat of mere rhymed prose. One of the longer, upon 'Enthusiasm,' may be mentioned as symptomatic of an often noticed transformation of meaning. Our ancestors understood by 'enthusiasm' the state

of mind of the fanatical sects of the Commonwealth, or of the 'French Prophets' of the
eighteenth century. An enthusiast meant a
believer in a sham inspiration. The gradual
change of the word to a complimentary meaning
marks the familiar change which was also shown
by the development of sentimentalism in literature. Byrom, following Law pretty closely, takes
'enthusiasm' to mean devotion to some end, and
is good or bad according to the goodness or
badness of the end. Everybody must have some
aim. The enthusiasm which Byrom shared with
Law meant a serious belief in Christianity, and
the worldly only scoffed because they were equally
enthusiastic about some really inferior aim. A
few verses will show how far Byrom could follow
in the steps of Pope. Expanding a sentence of
Law's, he compares the classical enthusiast with
the Christian. The mere scholar is grieved when
he sees

> Time, an old Goth, advancing to consume
> Immortal Gods and once eternal Rome ;
> When the plain Gospel spread its artless ray,
> And rude, uncultured Fishermen had sway;
> Who spared no Idol, tho' divinely carved,
> Tho' Art and Muse and Shrine-engraver starved;
> Who saved *poor wretches* and destroyed, *alas!*
> The vital marble and the breathing brass.

Where does all Sense to him and Reason shine?
Behold, in Tully's rhetoric divine!
'Tully!' Enough; high o'er the Alps he's gone,
To tread the ground that Tully trod upon;
Haply, to find his statue or his bust,
Or medal green'd with Ciceronian rust;
Perchance, the Rostrum—yea, the very wood
Whereon this elevated genius stood.
When forth on Catiline, as erst he spoke,
The thunder of '*Quousque tandem*' broke.

Byrom is beginning to forget even Tully's merits as a shorthand writer. He follows Law towards the condemnation, not only of the stage, but of classical scholarship and art in general.

It does not appear, however, that Byrom ever got quite so far. Law retired to his curious hermitage at King's Cliffe, where he could abandon himself to pious meditation and the demoralisation of the neighbourhood by profuse charity. Byrom was held fast by his domestic ties; and took an interest in the local politics of Manchester. His talent for versification gave him frequent employment. He contributed a number of verses, in the nature of election squibs, to a newspaper of the period, and whenever he has an argument with a friend, he twists his logic into verse. Some of the results are quaint enough. Tempted, apparently, by Bentley's example, he had made a variety of conjectural emendations of Horace, obviously rash, if not altogether absurd. But it could have entered into no less whimsical head to put the arguments for them into rhyme. He suggests *unum* for *nonum* in the familiar passage,

> I take the correction, *unumque prematur*,
> 'Let it lie for one twelvemonth'—Ah, that may
>   hold water!

and argues the point through twelve eight-lined stanzas. Another 'poem' is an antiquarian discussion, showing that St. Gregory and not St. George was the patron saint of England ; he proves in another that the locusts eaten by the Baptist were fruit, not insects ; in a third, that the miracle at the Pentecost was worked upon the hearers, not the speakers.

> 'Are not these,' said the men, the devout of each land,
> 'Galileans that speak, whom we all understand ?'
> As much as to say, 'By what wonderful powers
> Does the tongue Galilean become to us ours ?'

With equal readiness he enters into an elaborate exegetical discussion, defending Sherlock against Conyers Middleton ; expounds the orthodox doctrine of the fall of man and justification by faith ; condemns Jonathan Edwards's arguments

upon free-will, or versifies some prayer or letter
that has struck him in reading memoirs or
treatises of mystical divinity. The worthy
Byrom, it must be added, did not take his own
performances in this line too seriously. They
were an amusement—a quaint whim characteristic
of an oddly constituted brain ; and one fancies
that when he forces even Hebrew and Greek into
the fetters of his ' cantering rhymes,' and twists
dry grammatical discussion into comic metres,
he feels that the process takes the bitterness out
of controversy and enables him to treat thorny
subjects in a vein of pleasantry. It is characteristic that he came into collision with the colossal
Warburton, who had treated Law with his usual
brutality, and that even Warburton found it
desirable for once to be civil to so amiable an
antagonist.

Byrom's activity in the shorthand business
declined after the death of his brother in 1740
gave him the family estates. In 1745 he was
presented to the Chevalier in Manchester ; but
luckily did not commit himself in any dangerous
way to answering his own question, Which was
King and which was Pretender? Byrom was
very near the Quakers in such matters. In a

poem on the occasion his hero, representing
Lancashire in dialect and common-sense, decides,
in spite of patriotic taunts, to look after his own
carcass and leave Highlanders and redcoats to
fight it out. Byrom obviously approves. Nobody, as other poems prove, could be less given
to the worship of Jingo. He tried vainly to save
some young friends, less prudent than himself,
convicted of joining the rebels—and, of course,
wrote his petition in verse. He protested, too,
in verse, and with equal want of success, against
the denunciators of Admiral Byng. He died a
few years later (1763). He was not buried as
the law directed, in woollen. His executors had
to pay £5 as a fine. As Byrom does not appear
to have left any verses to justify the failure, we
may perhaps assume that the omission was not due
to any final whim of his own. He would hardly
have missed such a chance for a poem. Few
kindlier men have been buried either in woollen
or linen.

JOHNSONIANA [1]

DR. BIRKBECK HILL has completed his labours upon Johnson's life by publishing this collection of *Johnsonian Miscellanies.* He thanks only too warmly the person who had the good fortune to suggest this scheme. The suggestion, it must be said, needed very little originality. When Croker published his edition of Boswell's life, he saw that it would be desirable to gather the anecdotes from other sources. With curious infelicity, he at first thrust them into Boswell's text; but in later issues they appeared in a separate volume. For that performance Croker, in spite of the criticisms of Macaulay and Carlyle, deserves the thanks of all true Boswellians. Dr. Birkbeck Hill has now given his own collection, which necessarily coincides in great part with Croker's. He has, moreover, added to it a full apparatus of notes, indexes, and references to the original sources.

[1] *Johnsonian Miscellanies,* arranged and edited by George Birkbeck Hill, D.C.L., LL.D. Oxford, 1897, 2 vols. 8vo.

He is, like every conscientious workman, incompletely satisfied with his own performance : he utters a kind of groan when he reflects upon the improvements which he might make even now if the book had not been definitively printed off. Undoubtedly every piece of human composition has its faults ; and a critic has excellent reasons for not contradicting a confession of shortcoming : it would be to admit that he may perhaps be blinder than the author. I will, therefore, not commit myself to the very unprofessional declaration that I have detected no shortcomings : but I will venture to say that the contributors to Johnson's biography would be bound to admit, if they could still take an interest in the subject, that their performances have been treasured up and annotated with a care and intelligence unsurpassed in any similar performance. To have Dr. Birkbeck Hill's ten volumes on one's shelves is not only to have one of those delightful collections into which one can dip at any moment with a certainty of bringing up some quaint and fascinating anecdote, but also to have it so well arranged that one can be sure of regaining any half-remembered passage. In regard to his last instalment, I will only venture to express one doubt. Dr. Birkbeck Hill had thought, he tells us, of giving extracts from Mme. d'Arblay's *Diary*. Reflection soon convinced him that the diary was 'too excellent a piece of work to be hacked in pieces'; he accordingly exhorts readers to go to the lady's book for themselves, especially if they wish to see Johnson's 'fun and comical humour and love of nonsense, of which,' as she says, 'he had about him more than almost anybody she ever saw.' Now Jowett, a most appreciative Johnsonian, told Dr. Birkbeck Hill that if Boswell had misrepresented Johnson upon any point it was precisely upon this: Boswell had, perhaps, made Johnson too much of the sage and philosopher, and too little of the 'rollicking King of Society.' If Boswell be really guilty of this omission, it is surely rather unfortunate not to have passages from the writer who has best supplied the deficiency. Mme. d'Arblay's *Diary* is undoubtedly a very charming book; but, after all, a diary by its nature lends itself to being read in fragments. Perhaps a closer examination might justify Dr. Birkbeck Hill's conclusion; but one would be inclined to say on the first impression that room might have been found for Mme. d'Arblay by excising some heavier and less relevant matter.   Perhaps Johnson's 'Prayers and Meditations,' not here quite in their place, might have made way for samples of his fun.

The problem indeed which the book principally suggests concerns this question of the completeness of the Boswellian Johnson.   To some of us—I suspect, indeed, to a good many—Boswell represents the original source not only of knowledge about Johnson, but of our knowledge of English literature in general.   He was our introducer to the great anonymous club formed by English men of letters from the days when Shakespeare met Ben Jonson to the days when Carlyle discoursed to Froude.   We became members of the craft in spirit under Boswell's guidance, whether we have or have not become actually identified with it in the flesh.   It therefore becomes next to impossible to abstract from Boswell : all our later knowledge has been more or less ingrafted upon him, however far we may have travelled from the source : Boswell gave the nucleus : and more or less consciously we have used his world as a standard inevitably taken into account in all later judgments.   To suppose Boswell non-existent is for such readers to suppose a kind of organic change in our whole estimate of literary charac-

teristics. When reading, especially about some of
the other famous talkers, Coleridge's monologues
or Sydney Smith's explosions of fun, I find myself
thinking how they would have sounded at the
Mitre or the Turk's Head. Thanks to Boswell, I
take the Johnsonian article to be a fixed datum
like the official yard at the Tower; and to be
asked to put that out of my head is to be invited
to deprive myself of my only measuring-rod. It
is exceedingly difficult, at any rate, to put oneself
outside of Boswell and to construct a portrait of
Johnson simply out of such other materials as are
here put together. I have read Hawkins and
Mrs. Piozzi and the rest, but always with the
help of the preconceived notions. Where they
could be fitted into Boswell, I have accepted them
as corroborations; but when they differed, I have
probably rejected the uncongenial elements, with
a perhaps careless assumption that they must be
inaccurate. And yet, it seems only justice to
these respectable persons to consider whether we
ought not to reopen the point. If Mme.
d'Arblay saw something of Johnson which was
not revealed to Boswell, may we not discover
similar supplementary hints in the other attempts
at portraiture?

Johnson's life confirms one remark which is painfully impressed upon most readers of biography. A really first-rate biography ought, one may plausibly argue, to be the rarest of books. A man can write a poem by himself; but a biography requires not only a capable artist and a good subject, but the rare combination of circumstances which brings them together under the proper conditions. The most interesting part of most men's lives—and Johnson was no exception—is the early struggle in which their faculties were developing and the victory being won. A man, too, as Johnson said to Mrs. Piozzi, 'commonly grows wickeder as he grows older'; he would always, he declared, take the side of the young in a dispute, 'for you have at least a chance of virtue till age has withered its very root.' So far as my personal experience has gone, I think that Johnson was too nearly right. At any rate, the period of aspirations and illusions is the most interesting. Yet if a man lives to a full age, the companions of his youth are mostly dead; and the survivors, if by some fortunate chance there be any who are capable of articulate story-telling, look back too sadly and too bitterly on the old days to restore the old impressions to life.

Happy, in this respect at least, are those who die young. Die before you are forty and you may have friends capable of describing you at your best and freshest. But, as generally happens, Johnson's early friends had passed away long before his death. Except from incidental suggestions in his life of Savage and a few stray anecdotes, we have no vivid impressions of the period in which he was struggling for employment on *The Gentleman's Magazine* or slaving at the *Dictionary*, and still cheered by the presence of his wife. Johnson himself once suggested the names of one or two friends who could tell his future biographers about his early life. They were such as that worthy ' squarson' (in Sydney Smith's phrase), Dr. Taylor, in whom even Boswell could only once detect something like a sparkle of wit, and that of most doubtful quality. The professional biographer knows too well by sad experience what is the kind of information to be extracted from such sources : probably a couple of utterly pointless anecdotes, which he is forced to insert because he has asked for them, and which introduce some hopeless jumble of dates and facts. Johnson would not have been more than actually unfortunate if his sole official

biographer had been such a one as Sir John
Hawkins, of whom it is recorded by his venerated
friend that he was 'an honest man at bottom';
though, 'to be sure, he is penurious, and he is
mean, and it must be owned he has a degree
of brutality and a tendency to savageness that
cannot easily be defended.'   His rivals, who
agreed in little else, agree in their judgment of
Hawkins.   We may explain away Boswell's
antipathy: 'Hawkins,' he writes to his friend
Temple, 'is, no doubt, very malevolent. *Observe
how he talks of me "as quite unknown"!*'
Boswell, according to Miss Hawkins, wished to
be described as 'The Boswell,' whereas he had
only appeared as 'a native of Scotland.' Hawkins's
meanness and malignity, however, are asserted on
less suspicious evidence.   He was turned out of
the club for rudeness to Burke.   Jeremy Bentham
calls him a 'good-for-nothing fellow,' who was
always wondering—which Bentham oddly seems
to regard as an inconsistency—at the depravity of
other people.   The amiable Bishop Percy called
him a 'most detestable fellow': and the suave
Reynolds told Malone that he was not only 'mean
and grovelling' but 'absolutely dishonest.' He
tried to cheat Johnson's black servant, Barber,

out of a watch which his master had given to him
when dying; and thereby came in for some
stinging ridicule from Porson. Hawkins, indeed,
was grievously scandalised by Johnson's liberal
bequest of an annuity to Barber; and the more
so, one guesses, because it seems to have been
only through Hawkins's importunity that Johnson
was induced to make a will at the last moment.
A man who succeeded in combining the censures
of Johnson, Burke, Reynolds, Bentham, and
Porson, to say nothing of Boswell, Malone, and
Murphy, must certainly have had his weaknesses.
Yet Johnson had a kindness for him; and one
rather guesses that, after all, he was nothing worse
than an unusually dull, censorious, and self-
righteous specimen of the British middle-class of
his time. His most characteristic saying is that
Fielding was the 'inventor of a cant phrase,
goodness of heart, which means little more than
the virtue of a horse or a dog.' A good man is
one who can see the wickedness of Tom Jones
and fully appreciate the virtues of Blifil. Now, if
Johnson had died at the age of fifty-four or fifty-
five, Hawkins, had he condescended to undertake
the task, would have had no rivals in writing a
biography, and we should have been duly grateful

to him. For even in his very dingy and distort-
ing mirror we should have caught sight of a
grotesque, but impressive figure, an uncouth
Dominie Sampson, who, without Boswell, would
indeed be puzzling but would still show touches
of the familiar qualities.   Hawkins was dimly
aware, for example, though he cannot give proofs,
that Johnson could be humorous, and tells one
anecdote of the 'high jinks' which, by Boswell's
era, had become impossible.   When Mrs. Lennox
published one of her immortal novels in 1751,
Johnson induced Hawkins—with a shudder—to
'spend a whole night in festivity.'   A party of
twenty sat up at the Devil's Tavern : where there
was a 'magnificent hot apple-pye' stuck with
bay leaves—'because, forsooth, Mrs. Lennox had
written verses'—nay, 'Johnson encircled her
brows' with laurel, and performed ceremonies of
his own invention, and kept it up till morning.
At the dawn of day, his face 'still shone with
meridian splendour'—reminding us of a famous
performance of Socrates, though Johnson supported his spirits by lemonade instead of wine,
and the conversation was more proper than that
at the Platonic Symposium, if hardly so brilliant.
Poor Hawkins, however, slunk off about eight

with a 'sensation of shame' at the resemblance which the night's entertainment bore to a 'debauch.' He had the strength of mind to overcome these misgivings, and even to give this little narrative, and defy any doubts which it might suggest as to his own dignity. There was nothing, he is anxious to make us understand, which would have shocked even that reverent admirer of the 'dixonary,' Miss Pinkerton of Chiswick Mall. For the most part, it must be admitted, Hawkins has such readers before his eyes, and Johnson is with him the great moralist and author of the *Rambler*, whom M. Taine found—no wonder—to be unreadable. From Hawkins taken alone, we might have dimly divined aspects of the Boswellian Johnson; but, on the whole, the lexicographer would have been little more than a fine specimen of the old denizens of Grub Street. His discourse, says Hawkins, was of the 'didactic kind, replete with original sentiments expressed in the strongest and most correct terms.' Yet even Hawkins cannot quite damp the genuine fire in a few specimens which he has preserved.

Among the earlier friends we must reckon one incomparably superior person. Reynolds knew

Johnson from about 1754, and gives his impressions in two imaginary conversations. These, which were first published by Croker, are of very great interest. One would like to know, indeed, whether they were written in complete independence of Boswell ; for the coincidence is close and curious. They are meant to illustrate Reynolds's own remark, that Johnson considered Garrick to be his property, and would allow no one either to praise or to blame him without contradiction. No doubt Reynolds and Boswell had heard Johnson's comments often enough to account for a common element ; and, in any case, the similarity implies a valuable corroboration of Boswell's perspicuity. Reynolds, we may be sure, had a good eye for character, and looked at Johnson from the position of an equal, not a hero-worshipper. Yet the general result is the same, though the sharpness of the impression is naturally much greater in Boswell's verbal report. So, speaking of Garrick's being unspoilt by the attentions of great men, Johnson is made to say by Reynolds, that ' it is to the credit of Garrick that he never laid claim to this distinction. It was as voluntarily allowed as if it had been his birthright. In this I confess I looked on David with some degree of envy, not so much for the respect he received as for the manner of its being acquired. What fell into his lap unsought, I have been forced to claim,' and so on. In Boswell, Johnson remarks that Garrick had had applause 'dashed in his face, sounded in his ears, and went home every night with the plaudits of a thousand in his *cranium*. Then, Mr. Garrick did not *find* but *made* his way to the tables, the lives, and almost the bedchambers, of the great. If all this had happened to me, I should have had a couple of fellows with long poles walking before me, to knock down everybody that stood in the way.' Obviously the substance is the same ; but Johnson's words, in passing through the medium of Reynolds's bland and decorous interpretation, have lost all the vivid concrete imagery that fixes them in our memory. Johnson's only recorded blush was on the occasion of having said something rude to Reynolds ; and we can easily believe that the Reynolds atmosphere would soften and occasionally emasculate the pithy utterances of his friend. Reynolds's painted portraits of ' Blinking Sam ' show a power of interpreting the outward appearance which no doubt indicates a keen perception of the character beneath. But on reading his portrait in words, we feel that in some cases a photographic likeness is incomparably more effective than a judiciously toned and harmonised study by an ambitious artist. An interesting appendage to this paper gives the recollections of Sir Joshua's poor trembling sister Frances. When Boswell tried to get some of Johnson's letters from her, her 'too nice delicacy' prevented her compliance. She was ambitious enough to write some little poems, which Johnson assured her were 'very pretty,' and had much moved him. Considering that in the ten first lines she makes 'come' rhyme to 'prolong,' 'steep' to 'meet,' and 'averse' to 'redress,' one is not surprised that, though Johnson advised her not to burn them, he did not persuade her to publish them. The *Recollections*, though prepared for publication, also stayed in her desk. They show quaintly the impression made by Johnson on the nerves of the shrinking poetess. She was pleased at their first interview by hearing him tell how, when he went home at two in the morning, he would put pennies into the hands of children sleeping in the streets, that they might buy a breakfast when they awoke. She gives various anecdotes of kindness which he

had showed—as in giving her advice in such a
delicate matter as her difficulties with her famous
brother. But she had a struggle. He was, she
says, 'in affections mild,' but could not be called
'in manners gentle.' His celebrity, she thinks,
was 'sublimated, as one may say, with terror and
with love.' He was very rarely or never 'inten-
tionally asperous' (Miss Reynolds has some
delightful phrases), unless in defence of religion
or morality : but he 'inverted the common forms
of civilised society.' Miss Reynolds looks upon
him as a monstrous combination—a sage, if not a
saint, confined by a strange freak of nature in the
outside of a Caliban. Nobody, accordingly, has
given more singular accounts of his amazing
appearance : especially his performance of what
she calls his 'straddles.' She tells how he would
suddenly contort his feet into a geometrical
diagram, while his hands were raised as high as
possible above his head, or apparently meant to
imitate a jockey at full speed ; how, when he
passed through a door, he would whirl poor blind
Miss Williams about as he whirled and twisted in
his gesticulation, or else leave her groping outside
while he made a spring across the threshold,
apparently attempting (in modern phrase) to

establish a record for jumping. When Miss Reynolds took a walk with him in Twickenham meadows, he collected a crowd by these 'extraordinary antics,' and afterwards seesawed so violently while reading Grotius's *De Veritate* that people came up to ask what was the matter. Dr. Campbell also declares that Johnson looked like an idiot, without a rag of sense, and was 'for ever dancing the devil's jig,' or making a drivelling effort to 'whistle in his absent paroxysms.' No other biographer speaks so strongly of these amazing performances; and probably they had got upon Miss Reynolds's nerves. She amiably wishes to explain his apparently 'asperous' conduct; and certainly a man who was half deaf, so blind, as she declared, that he could not recognise a friend's face half a yard off, and, moreover, liable to become at any moment a mere bundle of automatic contortions, might be expected to tread on other people's toes, literally and metaphorically, without bad intentions. The 'two primæval causes,' as Miss Reynolds has it, his 'intellectual excellence' and his 'corporeal defects,' made him apparently harsh. The corporeal defects 'tended to darken his perceptions of what may be called propriety and impropriety in general conversation,' and the intellectual force made him hit hard. Miss Reynolds, no doubt, is speaking to the point ; but it is plain, too, that she would be horror-struck rather than amused whenever Johnson descended from his pedestal of the Rambler. He is still with her a heap of contradictory qualities.

Murphy was another friend of about the same period, whose essay is very properly reproduced here. It would make a respectable article in a biographical dictionary; but does not get beyond the humble merits attainable in such works. It was not till Johnson had emerged from his struggles and was reposing under the shelter of his passion that he at last met the predestined biographer. Boswell met him on 16th May 1763, and Mrs. Piozzi (Mrs. Thrale) 11th January 1765. Of the two, Mrs. Piozzi had certainly the best opportunities, and, indeed, opportunities better than those which have come to the most famous of biographers. Lockhart had not seen so much of Scott nor Froude of Carlyle. Both Lockhart and Froude, however, had the advantage of abundant material. They could tell the earlier story in the words of their own heroes; though in both cases the literary skill which turned the materials to

account was of the highest order.   Johnson's later
correspondence is characteristic enough, but only
a few fragments survive to cast an occasional gleam
of light upon the earlier period.   In the main,
therefore, the interest has to depend, not upon the
narrative, but upon the fully developed character.
We have to infer what Johnson was by our knowledge of what he became.   Mrs. Piozzi, naturally,
did not attempt a biography.   She was with her
second husband in Italy when she put together
from memory the collection of anecdotes which,
after Boswell, is, with all shortcomings, the nearest
approach to a satisfactory portrait of Johnson.
Mrs. Piozzi's book was a thorn in the flesh to
Boswell, who, however, has frequently the pleasure
of chuckling over some demonstrable inaccuracy.
She has been made into a kind of devil's advocate
in the case of Johnson's canonisation.   Hayward,
in his life of her, took her part in the famous
quarrel.   He had, of course, no difficulty in
pointing out that the British prejudices roused by
her second marriage were not justifiable in the
court of pure reason.   An Italian musician is
certainly not in the nature of things inferior to an
English brewer.   Piozzi appears moreover to have
been a real gentleman though he was a fiddler and

a foreigner; and, therefore, it must be fully granted that the wrath of Johnson and other friends, including her own daughters, at Mrs. Thrale becoming Mrs. Piozzi was absurd from a philosophical point of view. How far it was excusable, when we consider the social atmosphere of the time, need not be considered. The fact remains that the anecdotes are coloured by the intention. Nobody, I think, can doubt that the real cause of alienation was Mrs. Piozzi's knowledge that the marriage, rightly or wrongly, would offend her own circle, and, above all, would shock her revered monitor. She is, therefore, inclined to dwell upon the 'asperous' side of Johnson's performances, and to argue that the yoke which had been bearable when it was shared by Thrale became altogether intolerable when she had to support it by herself. Comparison with her own journals shows that this view, which is insinuated throughout, did not really correspond to the facts. It was not Johnson's mode of devouring his 'pudden,' or his rough speeches about Mrs. Thrale's sentimentalisms, which became suddenly inexcusable, but the way in which he showed his contempt for Piozzi. Granting this, however, the book, if a book 'with a tendency,' is still an admirable supplement to

Boswell; though it is now chiefly interesting as a
measure of Boswell's skill.   We need not inquire
whether the anecdotes told by both are given most
accurately by one or the other ; whether he told
Hannah More to consider what her flattery was
worth, before she choked him with it, or more
gently entreated the 'dearest lady,' after many
deprecations, to consider its value before she
'bestowed it so freely' ; or whether he told Mrs.
Piozzi that the world would be none the worse,
or that she would not herself be much concerned,
if all her relations were spitted like larks and
roasted for Presto's supper.   Was he ridiculing
her feeling or reproving her levity?   We can
never know for certain, but we can see clearly
enough in other cases which reporter can tell a
story most artistically.   Some of Boswell's critics
speak as though his only merit were in his
accuracy.   He had the courage, though his contemporaries gave it uglier names, to take out his
notebook and set down the words at the instant
when they dropped from Johnson's lips.   He
realised, though in a queer way, the immense
value of a contemporary note, and was as great
a reformer in biography as Gibbon in history.
That undoubtedly was a merit, especially at the

time when biographers in general thought it a duty
even to alter such contemporary documents as
they had ; and to give without warning, as Mason
did in the case of Gray, or even Lord Sheffield in
the case of Gibbon, not the actual letter, but a
compound of different letters.   Even Boswell
indeed, as appears from his notebook, thought
himself at liberty to touch up phrases, though
he may have thought that he was bringing
rough notes nearer to the truth.   But it is plain
that this was only one condition of his success.
Most proverbial good sayings, one is inclined to
suspect, are partly due to the reporters, or rather
to generations of reporters.   They have been
smoothed and polished like pebbles on a beach by
continuous attrition in the mouths of men, and if
we could see them in their original enunciation
they would be comparatively rough and clumsy.
On the other hand, the detached witticism loses,
and may entirely change, its significance when
taken as an isolated gem.   The special skill of
Boswell is in his power of giving, not the felicitous
phrase by itself, but the dramatic situation in
which it was struck out, and to which, even in its
unpolished state, it owed its impressiveness.   In
that he is not only superlative but, I fancy,

unique. There are countless collections of 'anas' and 'table-talks' from which we get some impression of the good things said by famous men. There are imaginary conversations which are sometimes admirable, even though we perceive, as we read them, that no real conversation was ever so continuous, or logical, or polished. Boswell seems to be alone in the art of presenting us in a few lines with a conversation which is obviously as real as it is dramatic. We listen to Johnson, but to Johnson surrounded by Garrick and Goldsmith and Burke and Wilkes, and appreciate not only the thing that was said, but what gave it point and appropriateness at the time, and under the circumstances. The fact was, of course, made possible by the nature of the Johnsonian circle. There are many admirable sayings in the table-talk of Coleridge, but a report of the whole would have obviously given us nothing but a diluted and discursive lecture. Carlyle's talk would have been in the same relation to his *Reminiscences* or his *Latter-day Pamphlets*. But Johnson's talk was superior to his writings, just because it was struck out in the heat of 'wit combats' with a circle which, even if it took the passive part of mere sounding-board, was essential to the effect. No one, however, except the inimitable Boswell clearly saw this or was able to turn the remark to account. Mrs. Piozzi gives us good things, but they are detached and discontinuous. She reports the phrases which for one reason or other had happened to stick in her memory. She is evidently eking out her recollections by bits of written Johnsonese. Johnson might perhaps have written in the *Rambler*, but could never have said in talk, that certain people are 'forced to linger life away in tasteless stupidity, and choose to count the moments by remembrance of pain instead of enjoyment of pleasure.' She probably gives an unintentionally false colouring to some of the sayings ; and, in any case, is unable to make a harmonious blending of the various elements. She remembers every now and then that Johnson was, on her showing, to be a man of the highest virtue ; and she proceeds to tell us how much he felt for the poor ; or how sorry he could be when he found that he had wounded a man's feelings unintentionally, or what excellent advice and help he would give to friends who were really in want of it. Mrs. Piozzi, however, being a singularly quick and vivacious lady, with a sarcastic and occasionally cynical turn, and no very profound appreciation of character, just stitches her anecdotes together as they come, and does not trouble herself to blend them into a consistent whole.

The more we read, in short, the more sensible we become of the unique merits of our old friend. He is far too familiar to justify any elaborate analysis of character, but a word or two may help to explain how his superiority to his rivals arose from his strange idiosyncrasy. The letters to Temple, first published in 1857, show the man even more distinctly than the life of Johnson ; and I have sometimes wondered that so curious a book has not been more generally read. As a self-revelation it is almost equal to a fragment of Pepys. Pepys was secretive enough to keep his diary to himself, whereas Boswell seems to have been equally willing to confide all his weaknesses to a friend. That quality, whatever it may be, seems to have been omitted from his composition which makes most people feel the absolute necessity of a veil of privacy. They have feelings of which they are not ashamed, but which it would be agony to expose to the gaze of their neighbours. Boswell seems to have enjoyed laying bare everything that he felt ; he would apparently have wished his confessor, if he had had one, to publish his avowals in the papers. 'Not a bent sixpence cares he,' as he says of himself in a boyish song, 'whether with him or at him you laugh.' To good-natured people there was something attractive in the confidingness which is implied in all his absurdities. Whether he introduces himself to the hero Paoli, the moralist Johnson, or to Mitchell, then the English Ambassador at the Court of Frederick, he immediately proceeds to give him full information as to the state of his soul. No other human being could have proposed that the great Chatham should 'honour him with a letter now and then,' in order to keep him 'ardent in the pursuit of virtuous fame.' He was at the time only known to Chatham as the author of the book upon Corsica, but thought it perfectly natural that the magnificent statesman should become his confidential adviser. Many distinguished people besides Johnson seem to have been flattered by his almost pathetic trust in their benevolence. His simplicity and good-nature were so unmistakable that, as Burke put it, they scarcely seemed to be virtuous. People overlooked the

impudence in consideration of the genuine good-
will.   David Hume and Wilkes seem to have felt
the charm as much as Johnson and Burke.   A
man who takes you into his confidence so frankly
is at least paying you a compliment.   It was only
such fine gentlemen as Walpole and Gibbon,
who stood upon their dignity and would not take
liberties even upon invitation, lest liberties should
be taken with them, whom Boswell found intolerable.   Gibbon in particular was an 'ugly, affected,
disgusting fellow,' who 'poisoned' the club for
him.   Still worse, indeed, were the people who
saw in Boswell's simplicity a chance of making
him a butt for rough practical jokes.   The
sycophants who surrounded his patron, Lord
Lowther, and the Bar of the Northern Circuit
seem to have embittered the poor man's last years
by using him in that capacity.   His disposition,
in fact, was not conducive to success in practical
life.   Boswell was far too easy-going and too apt
to snatch at any indulgences which came in his
way to play an effective part in a game of rough-
and-tumble.   The characteristic result was that
Boswell became a kind of interested looker-on,
like a delicate boy at a rough public school,
who admires the games, though he cannot take

part in them, and worships the heroes. To his
own fancy he was a kind of Hamlet. He explains to Paoli, as he had already explained to
Mitchell, that he had 'intensely applied himself
to metaphysical research,' and got 'beyond his
depth.' He had thus become for ever incapable
of taking a part in active life. He was proud, as
we know, of his hypochondria; and though he
frankly confesses to less refined causes of most of
his fits, he always cherishes the belief that they
imply a philosophical temperament. He delights
in supposing himself to be puzzling over the
problems of fate and freewill. But he has not
the courage to be a thorough sceptic or pessimist.
At bottom, he feels the world to be infinitely too
enjoyable to admit of a gloomy solution; and so
his real solace is in day-dreaming. He is always
in imagination overcoming his difficulties and
rising to fame and fortune. In a very characteristic letter (in 1789), he explains all his troubles:
Pitt had been 'ill-advised enough' not to
patronise a 'man of my popular and pleasant
talents.' His wife was dying; his property
embarrassed; and he was induced to adopt Johnson's melancholy view of the vanity of human
wishes. And yet he is still full of 'projects to

attain wealth and eminence'; and observes that
he is always 'looking back and looking forward,'
and wondering 'how he will feel in situations
which he anticipates in fancy.' In Corsica he
sang *Hearts of Oak* to the natives, and fancied
himself 'a recruiting sea-officer, with his chorus
of Corsicans aboard the British fleet.' He rode
Paoli's own horse, decked with 'crimson velvet'
and 'broad gold lace,' and fancied himself for a
moment to be the idol of an enthusiastic population. He is always playing at being something
delightful. He makes a vow 'under a solemn
yew-tree,' in the garden of his friend Temple,
and becomes straightway a model of all the
virtues. True, he did not keep it 'religiously,'
but that was because 'a little wine hurried him on
too much.' He promises Paoli, however, that he
will take no wine for a year, and, having kept his
promise for three weeks at the time of writing,
feels that he is virtually a reformed character.
The queerest result of this strange muddle
between the ideal and the practical appears in
his letters to Temple upon his love affairs. He
writes an admirable panegyric upon marriage to
his friend, and remarks that he 'looks with horror
on adultery.' This, however, is part of a passage

in which he explains that he has an amiable
mistress who, unfortunately, has also a husband.
His clerical friend hereupon seems to have blamed
him for 'keeping another man's wife.' Boswell
is startled at the phrase. That was literally his
scheme, as he admits, but 'imagination represented it just as being fond of a pretty, lively
black little lady, who, to oblige me, stayed in
Edinburgh, and I very genteelly paid her expenses.'
A year later Temple gives him a 'moral lecture'
for some scrape into which he has fallen, and gets
for answer that Boswell's 'warm imagination
looks forward with great complacency on the
sobriety, the healthfulness, and the worth of his
future life.' His imagination retained this inestimable power up to the last, and it must be
admitted, would be an admirable consoler to a
feeble conscience. It told him one truth, however, in 1790 : namely, that he was writing what
would be, 'without exception, the most enter-
taining book' that his correspondent had ever
read. Too characteristically he had realised his
aspirations just when success became valueless.
But, as a rule, he is in the odd position of one
who lives in a dream world, and yet one whose
dreams are always a version of realities.

Boswell is thus always playing at being something else, a melancholy philosopher or a virtuous judge or patriot; when he heard music, as he told Johnson, he felt himself 'plunging into the thick of the battle'; and after too convivial an evening, he retired in imagination to the deserts and adopted Rousseau's ideal 'savage state.' Still, as nobody appreciated more heartily the actual and solid pleasures of life, he could never detach himself from the world, though he did become disqualified for success. He could always restore his complacency by virtuous resolutions, and the friendship of good-natured people, and roamed through Vanity Fair lingering at every booth and distracted between the charms of every variety of enjoyment. He was precisely in the humour, therefore, to become a disciple of Johnson. For Johnson was the professor of a science which at that period was most flourishing. He was devoted, as he and his friends would have said, to the study of human nature. He was a 'moralist,' not meaning, as we might now mean, that he held any particular theories about 'hedonism' or 'self-realisation,' but that he was always observing concrete human beings, their eccentricities and miseries and varieties of character, with the eagerness of a scientific student. His favourite quotation, according to Mrs. Piozzi, was Pope's saying about the 'proper study of mankind.' The phrase, however, was taking a meaning rather different from that which it had borne in the days of Pope. The typical man of Pope's circle was to be found in Courts and at Ministers' levées. He was the person to be lectured upon manners by Chesterfield and initiated into Machiavellian worldly wisdom. Johnson, as the famous letter to Chesterfield shows, expressed among other things the intrusion of a new social element ; the rise of Grub Street to consideration, if not respect. He and his companions had known the world upon which Pope and his friends looked down with scorn, the world of sponging-houses and bailiffs and translators kept in Curll's garrets. The study of 'human nature,' as Johnson, and Fielding, and Hogarth, and their contemporaries understood it, had to take into account the life of London slums, and to consider a good many bald facts, coarse and repulsive enough, which their predecessors had regarded as beneath the notice of a gentleman. Dimly, too, they became aware of the passions which were leading, though they knew it not, to a great social upheaval, and beginning to be sentimental and denounce luxury and believe in the state of nature or the rights of man. Johnson was rich in such experience, and his best sayings are summaries of the reflections which it suggested. His reading and his criticism had all the same purpose. He loved biography and such history as deals with individual character. He could not bear to talk about the ' Punic War,' as he told Mrs. Piozzi—formal accounts of campaigns and conquests ; but he loved the history which showed 'how our ancestors lived.' He was even modern in his approval of early attempts to give accounts of 'common manners' rather than political events. He always estimates books, from Shakespeare to Richardson, by the 'knowledge of the human heart' which he considers them to contain. He loves London as a botanist might love a fertile country, on account of the abundance of the material for his favourite study. He sent Boswell and Windham to ' explore Wapping' on account of the variety of ' modes of life' to be found there. Boswell is generally ridiculed for his willingness to visit even such people as the famous Mrs. Rudd, who was probably guilty of forgery and something very like murder. Johnson would have visited her too, he said, if they had not already got into the habit of putting things into the papers ; and both would have justified themselves on the pretext that they were studying ' human nature.' When people go to Wapping now it is generally to carry out Mr. Charles Booth's admirable method of investigating great social problems. They deal with criminals by statistical tables, not by seeking the society of eminent murderers, or looking on at executions. We talk about sociology, not the study of human nature, and investigate the manners and customs of primitive savages instead of generalising our private personal experience. The speciality of Johnson's period is precisely this desire to consider the concrete human being, from Wapping to St. James's, as the subject-matter of a separate and intensely interesting science.

This, not to go further, characterises Boswell's view of Johnson. Boswell, already inclined to study life after a quaint and desultory fashion enough, to put himself in contact with all manner of famous people and to play their parts in imagination, imagined, not without excuse, that he had found in Johnson an embodiment of all the wisdom to be extracted from manifold experience of life, guided by profound penetration into character.   Johnson's conversation is delightful because it is full of the pithy aphorisms which concentrate the results of the experience. Johnson is the half-inspired prophet who can tell him what fruit to grow in his garden, what profession he should adopt, and how he should behave to his wife or his father.   If there were such a thing as a scientific knowledge of the human heart, and if Johnson had possessed it, there would be much sense in this ; and so far as strong common sense could be a substitute for science, Boswell was perhaps not so far wrong in his choice of an oracle.   It helps to explain— not Boswell's skill, for that is as inexplicable as all genius—but the special distinction between Boswell and his rivals.   Boswell, that is, had not only sat at the feet of the prophet, but had really imbibed his method.   The others, from Hawkins up to Mrs. Piozzi, simply take the point of view of the ordinary biographer.   They assume that their   readers   have   studied   *The Rambler*   or *Rasselas* or the *Dictionary*, and want to know something about the author.   They collect as many good sayings and characteristic anecdotes

as they can, and argue as to the justice of the
various charges of rudeness and so forth. Some
of them, who, from no fault of Dr. Hill's, fill
rather more pages than we could wish, think that
a great man ought to be mainly the hero of a
religious tract, and treat us simply to minute and
painful descriptions of the poor man's last days.
In any case, the real Johnson is for them the
author, and their function is simply to satisfy the
curiosity of his readers. Boswell being, in however quaint a fashion, a man of real genius, saw
instinctively something more. Johnson was, in the
first place, his oracle—the man who has extracted
the truth implicitly written in the book of human
life. But then, besides this, Johnson might also
be considered as himself a page in the book. To
understand his significance we must take not
merely his utterances, but their whole setting,
the 'environment' as well as the individual.
Boswell has to study the Johnson circle as he was
sent to study Wapping. Charing Cross is profoundly interesting because through it flows a full
tide of humanities. The biography is not merely
an account of Johnson, but what we should call
a study of human life. Johnson himself is, of
course, in the foreground—he was, so to speak,

a great nugget, a gigantic mass of 'human
nature.' He had that article, like Carlyle, in so
much abundance as to shock and alienate a good
many people who shrink from the rough ore,
however full it may be of precious metal. To
study him, therefore, was to study a type of surpassing interest, and nobody was really freer than
Boswell from what Macaulay, erroneously, I
should say, called the *lues Boswelliana*, the un-
qualified admiration even of a hero's failings. He
would not, as he told Hannah More, make his
lion a cat to please anybody, and perceived that
the shadows were necessary to do justice to the
lights. But the point in which he is even more
unique is the perception that Johnson, though
always in the foreground, is still to be only in the
foreground of a group of living and moving
human beings. The dramatic skill displayed in
such descriptions as the famous scene with Wilkes
enables him to do what is not even approached
by his rivals. It makes us incidentally share
Boswell's own feeling. He comes up from Edinburgh with such a 'gust' for London society as
excited even Johnson's wonder. It is not a mere
search for pleasure or amusement, but a kind of
scientific zeal, that animates him. He has a

genuine desire to see life at its fullest, all human passions stimulated to the utmost by the conflict of multitudes, and shown in the greatest variety by the mixture of men of all ranks and conditions, to see the keenest intellects of the day roused to activity by constant intercourse, and to have before his eyes every variety of incident, from a change of Ministry to a procession of criminals to Tyburn tree. The insatiable curiosity is only stimulated by the circumstance that he is jostled aside by men of stronger fibre and obliged to look on or to play his part by 'a warm imagination' instead of actual participation. This, I take it, is why Boswell's rivals seem to give us merely a collection of detached anecdotes, while in Boswell all the persons seem to come suddenly to life and give us a real insight into the whole social sphere instead of being mere lay figures. Mme. d'Arblay perhaps deserves the exception made in her favour, in so far as she has the real novelist's instinct, and gives us lively accounts of incidents, instead of isolated facts. But Mme. d'Arblay scarcely sees more than one aspect of Johnson—the famous old moralist who likes to make a pet of a charming young woman, and relaxes into more than usual playfulness in course of administering delightful doses of pardonable flattery. Of the others, even of Mrs. Piozzi, we can hardly say more than that they become amusing by the light of Boswell.   He has revealed the actors to us with such skill that even the dry and pompous narratives enable us to supply what was wanting, as in the dullest of reports we can sometimes hear the accents of a familiar friend.

NOTE.—Mr. Percy Fitzgerald has recently published a 'Critical Examination' of Dr. Birkbeck Hill's Johnsonian editions.   Mr. Fitzgerald refers more than once to the fact that I have been 'beguiled' into speaking of the edition of Boswell's *Life of Johnson* as the best known to me. Indeed, it seems that the edition has been very generally welcomed ; and Mr. Fitzgerald's severe criticism comes as a rather surprising discord in a general chorus of praise.   In any case, I feel it right to say a few words in defence of an opinion to which I confess that I still adhere without hesitation.   My reason is simple.   I have for years made constant use of the *Life of Johnson,* and have found Dr. Birkbeck Hill's notes exceedingly useful.   Whenever I am in want of information about any of the Johnson circle, I regularly turn for help to this edition, and I very seldom open it without gaining some light upon the matter in hand.   I think that I should have been ungrateful if I had not acknowledged so much ; and I will briefly state why I cannot retract my acknowledgment.   Mr. Fitzgerald criticises Dr. Birkbeck Hill for giving a great deal of irrelevant information, for frequently misunderstanding his author, and for frequent inaccuracy.   The first count depends more or less upon what seems to me to be a matter for fair difference of opinion.

I quite admit that Dr. Birkbeck Hill has given a quantity of information in his notes which has little or no direct bearing upon Johnson himself, or upon Boswell's discharge of his biographical duties. But I also confess that I have found such notes very pleasant reading, and been grateful for them. I like an occasional excursion into matters suggested by the text and illustrative of the period. If Mr. Fitzgerald does not like them, he has after all the simple remedy of not reading them. To give an example : Mr. Fitzgerald ridicules a note (Hill's *Boswell*, iii. 241) in which Dr. Birkbeck Hill illustrates by several quotations the curious change in the meaning of the word ' respectable.' Chesterfield speaks, for example, of the hour of death as ' at least a very respectable one,' and Hannah More thinks a roomful of portraits of admirals a ' respectable sight.' The note is certainly superfluous, but I am grateful for the knowledge conveyed in a few lines as to a really curious instance of the shifting of meaning in a familiar word. Dr. Birkbeck Hill, again, defends Johnson against Macaulay's statement that he knew nothing of the country, and despised travelling. In the course of his remarks he gives the populations of Lichfield, Oxford, and Birmingham, where Johnson spent most of his early life, to show that they were then small country towns, and points out that a boyish perusal of Martin's account of the Hebrides had stimulated the curiosity long afterwards satisfied by the journey with Boswell. Mr. Fitzgerald ridicules these statements, which occur in a disquisition in Appendix B to the third volume. No doubt they are not strictly necessary, but to me they really illustrate some of Johnson's characteristic prejudices, and qualify one of Macaulay's slashing assaults. I was again innocent enough to be grateful for them.

This suggests another point. Mr. Fitzgerald ridicules Dr. Birkbeck Hill's enormous and self-made index. Undoubtedly it errs, if anything, by excess. That is a very rare fault, and a fault on the right side. I have found the index

exceedingly useful on very many occasions, and been grateful
for the labour bestowed, which has often saved me a great
deal of trouble. The present occasion is an instance. Mr.
Fitzgerald has given hardly any references to the passages
which he criticises ; and I have had to find them by the help
of Dr. Birkbeck Hill himself. In some cases, I have been
unable to verify Mr. Fitzgerald's references even with that
help, and I am forced to suspend my judgment of his
criticisms. Thus (p. 13) he accuses Dr. Birkbeck Hill of
giving '*sixteen passages*' to illustrate the meaning of 'Hockley
in the Hole.' In the only passage which I can find about
'Hockley in the Hole' (vol. iii. 134), Dr. Birkbeck Hill
illustrates the meaning by quotations from the *Spectator*,
Fielding's *Jonathan Wild*, and the *Beggars' Opera*. That is,
there are only three passages cited, and, as it seems to me, not
one too many. But the absence of a reference leaves a bare
possibility that Dr. Birkbeck Hill has quoted other passages
elsewhere. Considering, however, the completeness of the
index, I believe that Mr. Fitzgerald has somehow made an
odd mistake in counting.

This is the more probable because I find other singular
mistakes, which show that Mr. Fitzgerald, in accusing his
author of inaccuracy—doubtless the worst of faults in an
editor—has himself been inaccurate with the passages before
his eyes, and his attention, one supposes, fully awake. At
page 4 he says that Dr. Birkbeck Hill's index proves that the
editor had never seen Boswell's first production—'certainly
never read it.' The 'proof' is that in the index it is mentioned
in italics as ' *The Club* ' at Newmarket. In the text, he adds,
it is again written 'the Club.' Now the real title was the
Cub, as any one must perceive who has read the book. I turn
to the index (vol. vi. p. 25), and there find *Cub at Newmarket*
correctly entered between 'critics' and 'curiosity.' I look
back to the text (vol. i. 383, n. 3), and there, it is true, the
word is written 'Club.' But as Dr. Birkbeck Hill quotes a

phrase from the preface, in which the Jockey Club at Newmarket is mentioned, I am charitable enough to believe that he
had really seen the book, and that 'Club' in the text is probably
a correction introduced by the excessive zeal of a reader misled
by the reference to the Club. At page 11, Mr. Fitzgerald comments upon a note in which Dr. Birkbeck Hill explains a passage in Johnson's letter on receiving the M.A. degree at Oxford
by referring to a seditious placard published during the period of
excitement over the famous Oxfordshire election of 1754. The
letter, says Mr. Fitzgerald, was written in February 1755, and
the placard appeared in 'July, five or six months later. So the
whole speculation topples over!' It would, were it not that the
placard appeared in July 1754 (not 1755), as is indeed obvious
from Dr. Birkbeck Hill's reference to the *Gentleman's Magazine*
of that year (vol. i. 282). At p. 16, Mr. Fitzgerald attacks Dr.
Birkbeck Hill's dates. Dr. Birkbeck Hill (vol. i. 146) says that
Johnson had his first interview with Hogarth 'sixteen years'
after coming to London. 'This cannot be accurate,' says
Mr. Fitzgerald. Why? The date of the interview is fixed
by its happening soon after the execution of Dr. Cameron
for his share in the '45. Therefore, Mr. Fitzgerald assumes,
it took place in 1745-6. If he had not been aware of
Cameron's well-known story, he might have found it in the
note before his eyes, where the date of the execution is
stated, namely, 7th June 1753. As Johnson came to London
in 1737, Dr. Birkbeck Hill is again quite right. I will
give one other strange proof of Mr. Fitzgerald's carelessness.
In the collection of Johnson's letters, Dr. Birkbeck Hill speaks
of Reynolds's prosperity in 1758. He gives, says Mr. Fitzgerald, an 'odd proof' of it, namely, that in 1758 Reynolds
had '150 letters': certainly this would be an odd proof of
prosperity; but in Dr. Birkbeck Hill's notes (vol. 1. 76 *n*.) the
words are '150 sitters'—a fact which most portrait-painters
would regard as a pretty good proof of prosperity.

I do not say that all Mr. Fitzgerald's criticisms are of this kind. He has discovered some real mistakes. The man who should publish ten volumes, elaborately annotated, without a mistake would be a wonder, and Mr. Fitzgerald is well qualified to find them. But I confess that to my mind the number discovered is so small as to confirm my belief in Dr. Birkbeck Hill's general accuracy; and, in any case, Mr. Fitzgerald has made too many slips to allow us to accept his opinion without careful examination. On some other points, I admit that Mr. Fitzgerald has a stronger case. I could not in any short space give my reasons for disputing many even of his more plausible remarks; but he has, no doubt, pointed to a weakness in the edition. The simple truth is, I take it, that Dr. Birkbeck Hill has ridden his hobby rather too hard. He has sometimes indulged in real irrelevance; remarks have occurred to him which he has inserted too hastily, and which he might have expunged on a more careful consideration of the text; he has made some wrong identifications; and has been led by associations, not shared by most of his readers, to expatiate here and there on needless topics. All this is the weakness of an enthusiast, and of a commentator who sometimes is over eager to say something when there is nothing to be said; or to discover difficulties which do not really exist. But, to my mind, the enthusiasm has also had invaluable results; it has given us an edition in which almost everything is to be found, though mixed with some superfluities. I wish that Mr. Fitzgerald had recognised this more warmly, and that all true lovers of Johnson and Boswell, to which class he undoubtedly belongs, could take advantage of what is good in each other's labours without being too anxious to dwell upon immaterial short-comings.

GIBBON'S AUTOBIOGRAPHY

Wᴇ are all grateful to Lord Sheffield for the publication of the original documents out of which Gibbon's *Memoirs of my Life and Writings* was constructed. It is curious to see a great work in its early stages, and the new matter thus presented helps to fill out and complete a picture sufficiently familiar in outline. The first Lord Sheffield had indeed done his work of editing and piecing together so well that there is little that amounts to a fresh revelation of character. The new volumes rather justify or strengthen than modify in any sensible degree the impression of the familiar book. Gibbon's characteristic good fortune has followed him even now. We see that the temporary suppression of the documents was as right as their ultimate publication. What would once have been superfluous or improper for publication is now interesting material for explaining the claim of a classical biography.

All critics agree that Gibbon's autobiography
is a model in its way. Every autobiography is
interesting, even when it unveils a mere time-
server and hypocrite like Bubb Dodington. It is
curious to know how a thoroughly mean nature
is justified to itself. Other memoirs, Coleridge's
Biographia Literaria for example, have a higher
interest, because they record the aspirations of men
of genius, who have yet wasted half their energy
through the caprices of fortune or misjudgment of
their own powers. But Gibbon's has the very
rare and peculiar charm of recording complete
success and what may in one sense be called
perfection of character. I do not mean to
attribute to Gibbon moral perfection in an absolute
sense. He had his little weaknesses, and anybody
who pleases may expatiate upon them for our
edification. By perfection I only intend perfection
relatively to a given purpose, and consequently
that peculiar balance or harmony of all the faculties
which enables a man to get the very greatest possible
result out of given abilities. Moralists may perhaps
maintain that there is properly only one ideal. I
will not argue the point. But as a matter of fact,
we may also say that there are many moral types,
each of which has its value, and may play a useful

part in the whole order of society. A career
which is a systematic application of a single
governing principle has at least an æsthetic, if
not a purely ethical, charm. It represents a
successful experiment worth noting in the great
art of life. The subject may not be a saint or a
hero—Gibbon certainly was neither—but under
some conditions he may achieve results of which
the saint and hero would be incapable. We may
prefer Chatham or Clive or Wesley to Gibbon ;
but if he had followed any of their examples, we
should have lost something which the whole
generation could not have supplied without him.
The course of intellectual development would
have been sensibly different. Gibbon's type, no
doubt, was the epicurean. Pleasure, he would
have frankly admitted, is the true end of life.
But pleasure to him, though it did not entirely
exclude the grosser elements, and might occasionally be sought even at a militia mess-table, or in
the more elegant dissipation at Almack's, included
a strenuous and ceaseless exertion of the intellect
upon worthy ends. It included, too, if not
romantic devotion, yet fidelity in friendship, and
the hearty enjoyment of the society of philosophers
and statesmen. A higher as well as a lower strain

of moral purpose would have disqualified Gibbon
for the one great work which he achieved.   Had,
in short, a superhuman being been required to fit
such an intellect with the character best able to
turn it to account or to fit the character with the
most appropriate intellect, he could not have
devised a better combination.   Comte prefixes to
his system of philosophy the motto from Alfred
de Vigny : *Qu'est-ce qu'une grande vie ? Une
pensée de la jeunesse exécutée par l'âge mûr.* Judged
by that test, Gibbon's life was of the greatest.   How
rare is the realisation of the maxim in any
department of life need hardly be said.   We have
just been congratulating Mr. Herbert Spencer
upon the conclusion of the labours of a lifetime
devoted to a single purpose.   There cannot, I
think, be too hearty a recognition of the great
moral qualities implied.   A retrospect of the history of philosophy would show how few are the
careers to be compared to it.   In poetry, Dante is
of course the great instance of complete achievement ; Milton too may be said to have carried
out in *Paradise Lost* the purpose of his youth ;
but the works even of our greatest poets are
mainly a collection of short flights instead of a
continuous evolution of a lifelong scheme.   In

history, Gibbon's great book stands almost alone in English literature.   The one British author of his own day whose work could in any department stand a comparison in these qualities was Adam Smith, whose *Wealth of Nations* appeared in the same year with the first volume of the *Decline and Fall*.   That, too, was the product of many years' concentrated effort upon a task early taken up. At the present day, if we take for granted the conventional lamentations, the chances of such achievement are smaller than ever.   We are, our sentimentalists complain, too hurried and jaded by the excitement of modern society to devote ourselves to a single purpose.   We ' fluctuate idly without term or scope ' ; and ' each half lives a hundred different lives ' Our works are fragmentary because we live in a perpetual hurry. We also suffer, indeed, from the opposite evil. Modern authors often contrive to write books quite long enough; and undertake sufficiently gigantic tasks.   Unfortunately, the vast accumulation of materials and the demand for exhaustive inquiry overpowers the conscientious writer, unless he be a German professor, and then is rather apt to extinguish his vivacity.

I am, I confess, rather suspicious of these

lamentations, but, without suggesting possible
answers or qualifications, they no doubt explain
one cause of the peculiar pleasure of transporting
ourselves to the middle of the eighteenth century,
when political revolutions and mechanical inventions had not yet turned things topsy-turvy.
When I indulge in day-dreams, I take flight with
the help of Gibbon, or Boswell, or Horace
Walpole, to that delightful period.   I take the
precaution, of course, to be born the son of a
prime minister, or, at least, within the charmed
circle where sinecure offices may be the reward of
a judicious choice of parents.   There, methinks,
would be enjoyment, more than in this march of
mind, as well as more than in the state of nature
on the islands where one is mated with a squalid
savage.   There I can have philosophy enough to
justify at once my self-complacency in my wisdom
and acquiescence in established abuses.   I make
the grand tour for a year or two on the Continent,
and find myself at once recognised as a philosopher
and statesman, simply because I am an Englishman.   I become an honorary member of the tacit
cosmopolitan association of philosophers, which
formed Parisian *salons*, or collected round Voltaire
at Ferney.   I bring home a sufficient number of

pictures to ornament a comfortable villa on the banks of the Thames ; and form a good solid library in which I write books for the upper circle, without bothering myself about the Social Question or Bimetallism, or swallowing masses of newspaper and magazine articles to keep myself up to date.   I belong to a club or two in London, with Johnson and Charles Fox, the authors and the men of fashion, in which I can 'fold my legs and have my talk out,' and actually hear talk which is worth writing down.   If I do not aspire to be one of the great triumvirate, of which Gibbon was proud to be a member, I fancy at least that I can allow my thoughts to ripen and mellow into something as neat and rounded as becomes a fine gentleman.

It is true, of course, that this plan involves certain postulates.   It might be that in the real eighteenth century I should have turned my opportunities to bad account.   I might become a mere dilettante or a mere sensualist. What is remarkable in Gibbon is the felicity with which his peculiar talents and temperament fitted in with the accidents of his life, as though by a specially devised arrangement.   It may be worth while to note in some detail the curious play of external circumstance and mental and moral constitution which went to produce this unique result; to observe how dexterously fortune combined all the external elements which were necessary to mould and direct a great historian. Much that looked like misfortune was an essential blessing in disguise; a fact which does not diminish Gibbon's credit for taking the hints in the right way. In his own summary he admits that he has 'drawn a high prize in the lottery of life.' A cheerful temper, equable though not vigorous health, and a 'golden mediocrity of fortune,' are the chief advantages which he enumerates. On the last circumstance he makes an instructive comment elsewhere. Wretched, he says, is the work of the man whose daily diligence has to be stimulated by daily hunger. The author of the splendid eulogium upon Fielding, the friend of Goldsmith and associate of Johnson, should perhaps have admitted that poverty was not of necessity paralysing. Yet it is true that no denizen of Grub Street could have produced such a work as the *Decline and Fall,* and that with Gibbon's delicacy of constitution life in that region would have been ruinous. A combination of wide research and leisurely reduction of chaotic materials into a well-

ordered whole would have been impossible for him
with a printer's devil always round the corner.
Had he had greater wealth, on the other hand—
had his grandfather not been ruined by the South
Sea speculation, or his father been capable of
retrieving instead of damaging his fortunes—
Gibbon would have been exposed to possibly fatal
temptations. He might have dissipated his
powers, and become a luxurious 'virtuoso,' like
Horace Walpole ; and he still more probably might
have been swept into the political vortex, the
temptations of which, as it was, were almost
fatal to the conclusion of the *History*. The class,
again, to which he belonged was, with all its faults,
accessible to the culture of the time ; and had
some excuse for considering itself to be leading
the van of European civilisation. England was
still held on the Continent to be the model land of
political and religious freedom ; and the French
philosophers who ruled the world of thought were
still sitting at the feet of Locke and Newton. It
is true that the education which a young Briton
received was not exactly calculated to produce
philosophers. Gibbon observes that 'a finished
scholar may emerge from the head of Westminster
or Eton in total ignorance of the business and

conversation of English gentlemen' of the period. All that was positively done was to instil a little grammar, at the expense of 'many tears and some blood.' A lad of spirit got some useful knowledge, as Gibbon thinks, and some, it is to be feared, by no means useful, from the rough freedom of the public schools. Gibbon's delicacy forced him to supplement his grammatical studies, not by boxing or cricket, but by reading. The grammar at least taught a thoughtful lad the value of accurate knowledge within a very narrow sphere. Meanwhile, at twelve he knew Pope's *Homer* and *The Arabian Nights* by heart; and at fourteen the future historian was already swallowing 'crude lumps' of Speed, Rapin, and many standard works on history and travel. He tells us how, at that period, he was 'immersed in the passage of the Goths over the Danube' when the dinner-bell dragged him from his intellectual feast. By the age of sixteen he had 'exhausted all that could be learnt in English of the Arabs and Persians, the Tartars and the Turks'; he was 'guessing at the French of d'Herbelot and construing the barbarous Latin of Pocock's *Albufaragius.*' A neglect which might have been fatal to others was just what Gibbon required; and the incapacity of his schoolmasters was one of the first fortunate elements in his surroundings.   It gives one a pang to think of the probable fate of a modern Gibbon.   Even ill-health would hardly save him from the clutches of the crammer ; or prevent so promising a victim from being forced upon the reflection that a knowledge of Turks and Tartars would not pay in a competitive examination.

Feeble health and the absence of all judicious training had thus enabled Gibbon to recognise, however dimly, the career for which he was predestined.   At first sight it would seem that the merits of Oxford in the way of neglect would be carried to excess.   Even here, such was the singular felicity of his life, the result was exactly what was required.   What would have happened to Gibbon if the tutor who 'remembered that he had a salary to receive, and only forgot that he had a duty to perform,' had put his memory to the proper use ?   Gibbon, who was essentially docile and placid by temperament, might easily have been made into a model pedant—a Dr. Parr or Tom Warton of monstrous erudition and inadequate performance.   He might have cherished a de-caying Jacobitism in comfortable, common rooms;

and, as he puts it, have sunk into the ' fat slumbers
of the Church.'   The deliverance came by the
most apparently unfavourable turn of fortune.
Gibbon's conversion to Catholicism appeared in
later life to himself and to others to be a mere
boyish freak.   He could only wonder how he had
ever believed such nonsense.   Of course the conversion of a lad just sixteen was a superficial process.   His imagination had not been swayed by
the æsthetic charm of the Church, nor did he
come as one wearied by sceptical wanderings and
longing for spiritual slavery.   He was apparently
the victim of a single argument, and convictions
so produced are easily modified.   But the argument was also curiously characteristic.   The lad
had been left to wander rough in theological as
other literature, guided only 'by the dim light
of his catechism,' and his omnivorous appetite for
all knowledge was stimulated by a contemporary
controversy.   Conyers Middleton was then making
a sensation resembling that created about a century
afterwards by *Essays and Reviews*.   The old
deistical movement in his hands was becoming
mainly historical instead of metaphysical.   It
raised, therefore, the great problem to which
Gibbon was substantially to devote his life.

The freethinker held that the Church had not, and had never had, miraculous powers; the Catholic that it had such powers formerly, and possessed them still; and the Protestant that the powers had disappeared at some date which it was rather difficult to fix.   To Gibbon the Protestant view seemed to be in any case illogical.   So it still seemed when he wrote the fifteenth chapter of his *History*.   As, however, he was not prepared to give up the miraculous power altogether, and as he knew enough to see that it was claimed long after some of the Catholic dogmas were current, he adopted the Church which held at least a consistent position.   Of the logic of this argument I say nothing; but its power over Gibbon is one more proof that he was a heaven-born historian.   He tells us that his own memory convinced him of the fallacy of the opinion held by Johnson and Reynolds that a man of ability could turn his powers in any direction.   His own idiosyncrasy was too unequivocal.   A poet may perhaps be content to think of the past as a region of romance and wonder; the born historian is one who feels instinctively that the men of old were governed by the laws which are operative now; he takes for granted, though unconsciously, the great doctrine of the continuity of history. Both the consummation and the start of Gibbon's career represented this instinctive conviction. He was already not only reading ecclesiastical history, but reading it as a record of real events, not as a mere compendium of dates and names. His great work was to bridge the interval between ancient and modern history; and his boyish understanding had already been impressed by the identity of the great institution which connects the two periods.

The most fortunate, perhaps, of all the turns of fate now followed. Gibbon's father was apparently not a great philosopher nor a very wise man; but he took, by a kind of dumb instinct, or through occult influence of the son's presiding star, the very best course that could have been taken. Gibbon's exile to Lausanne was meant to break off his old connections. It succeeded, and it placed him in a frugal and industrious circle, with no such distractions as tempted luxurious youths at Oxford. He could fairly devote his whole time to intellectual employment. The father had counted, apparently, upon the dialectical skill of the Swiss tutor. The 'intermixture of sects' had, as Gibbon remarks, made the Swiss clergy acute controversialists, and the worthy Pavillard pointed out to him the errors of the Church of Rome, proved that it could derive no authority from St. Peter, and that 'transubstantion' (as Gibbon calls it) was a modern fiction.   This may have been all very well ; but Pavillard, spite of a little vanity, was also a man of excellent sense, and saw that the true remedy was to stimulate Gibbon to reflect for himself, without obtrusively guiding his thoughts.   Gibbon expresses his wonder that no Catholic priest had been told off to keep the young convert from deserting the fold.   He might have been induced to make constancy to his creed a point of honour.   Fortunately, he had been touched by a more stimulating influence. The clergy of the Pays-de-Vaud had, as Gibbon says, become liberal under the influence of Crousaz, known to Englishmen chiefly as the assailant of Pope, a ponderous writer upon logic and a disciple of Locke.   Gibbon read Crousaz's logic and Locke's essay, and imbibed ideas un-known to, or dreaded by, the Jacobite dons at Oxford.   At Lausanne, moreover, he had the honour of introduction to the great Voltaire. Voltaire, indeed, appeared to him chiefly in the character of dramatist and actor.   Gibbon speaks with moderate enthusiasm of a man who, considered as a historian, necessarily seemed superficial and inaccurate to his critic. The names thus mentioned are enough to suggest what had really happened. Gibbon had ceased, as he tells us, to be an Englishman. French had become more natural to him than his own language; and his friends held that he had suffered 'a serious and irreparable' mischief. Gibbon had, however, become not a Swiss nor a Frenchman, but a cosmopolitan. He had been initiated into the freemasonry of the most enlightened circles of Europe. 'Whatever have been the fruits of his education,' he says, they 'must be ascribed' to his 'fortunate banishment.' Instead of being 'steeped in port and prejudice among the monks of Oxford,' he had breathed a larger air and had become familiar with the thoughts which were shaking the whole intellectual fabric of the time. He could look at history, not from an insular point of view, or in the interests of some narrow set of dogmas, but from the widest philosophical standing-ground of the period. For the present, indeed, history seems to have been rather in the background. He threw himself upon classical literature with an appetite which never failed him in later years.

He read the great authors, though his Greek still
remained imperfect; not for any narrow purpose,
but as one who is to make them bosom companions for life.   Cicero's writings first fascinated
him, and he read not only to appreciate the style,
but for the 'admirable lessons' of conduct 'applicable to almost every situation of public and private
life.'   Then, in twenty-seven months, he read
through nearly the whole of the Latin classics :
and, what is characteristic, his review 'though
rapid was neither hasty nor superficial.'   He
made abstracts, worked hard at difficult passages,
and followed out every subsidiary line of inquiry
which suggested itself.   He tells us at a later time
how, before reading a new book, he took a solitary
walk and reflected carefully upon the state of his
knowledge, that he might judge what benefit he
received from his author.   So he prepared himself
afterwards for his Italian journey, not by buying a
Murray's handbook—the reason is obvious—but
by writing a handbook for himself, in which were
collected all the classical passages bearing upon
the geography of the country.   To have all your
existing knowledge well arranged and thoroughly
in hand was, he felt, the best way to add to it.
Omnivorous reader as he was, he accepts the

principle *non multa, sed multum,* and made his
ground sure at every step.   In other words, he
had the true scholar's instinct, but duly controlled
by the philosophic turn for meditation upon
general principles.   He would indulge in minute
researches, but would never lose himself in the
multiplicity of details.   His mode of writing
shows the same perception.   He used, as he tells
us, to 'cast a long paragraph in a single mould,'
to 'try it by his ear,' and to 'suspend the action
of the pen till he had given the last polish to his
work.'   Most of us, I fear, think that we have
done enough when we begin a single sentence
with an approximate guess at the way of getting
out of it.   The man who composes by paragraphs
will also frame his chapters with a view to their
position in an organic whole.   The philosophy
into which Gibbon was initiated was congenial to
his method.   The great writers of the day asked,
above all things, for good, sweeping formulæ, and
they preferred such as could be packed into an
epigram.   The French influence, as Mr. Cotter
Morison remarks, was especially valuable.   A
Frenchman, whatever his faults, always recognises
the truth, too often forgotten elsewhere, that every
chapter of a book should be written with reference

to the whole.   There should be a central, animating idea.   Gibbon's own view is indicated in his
very interesting though crude French essay on the
study of literature, written (1758-59) at the
beginning of his literary career.   It was intended
to defend the doctrine—less needed, one might
have supposed, then than now—that literature
should not be dethroned by the mathematical and
physical sciences.   But he argues that a true
appreciation of literature demands wide knowledge
and thorough study.   He insists upon the close
connection of all branches of knowledge, and
declares that if a philosopher is not always a
historian, a historian should always be a philosopher.   He should be tracing the operation of
general causes.   He should deal with apparent
trifles; not out of mere curiosity or love of the
picturesque, but because they are often the clearest
indications of principles of wide application.   He
should inquire, for example, into the origin of
grotesque mythologies, and might even, as he
points out, find valuable hints in the moral
notions of an 'Iroquois.'   Though ill-arranged
and disjointed, the essay thus shows keen glimpses
into methods which have since assumed greater
importance.

So far, fate, acting upon Gibbon's idiosyncrasies, had prepared him for his great work. But his presiding genius had still to guard against various dangers. Gibbon might have rivalled the erudition of a German professor, and polished it with some of the skill of a French literary artist. But the historian wants something more : the infusion of practical instinct which comes from familiarity with actual affairs, and should give reality to his narrative. Gibbon was in a fair way to become a ' book in breeches '; his detachment from his own country had made him cosmopolitan, but it had left him a secluded student. He had formed his lifelong and invaluable friendship with Deyverdun, one of those rare and delightful associations which are only formed in youth and by close community of intellectual tastes. But Deyverdun ' hung loose upon society '; he and his friend aspired to be members of the literary world of Europe— but only as authors of a learned journal. They had no points of contact with business. How was Gibbon to be brought into contact with the real world, the world of passion and active interests, in which literature is a mere surface phenomenon, and yet to be initiated without being absorbed ? That represents a delicate problem which his fortune solved with singular felicity.

In the first place, of course, Gibbon must have the great experience of falling in love. It must be a passion strong and exalted enough to let him into the great secret of human happiness, and yet it must not be such as to entangle him too deeply in the active duties of life. A man who has never been stirred to such passion must look too much from outside upon the great drama of life ; and yet the passion, if sufficiently powerful, may lead him too far from his predestined functions. Mlle. Curclod was the appointed instrument of fate for solving this problem. She was beautiful and intelligent enough to rouse Gibbon to an apparently genuine devotion ; and yet as she was a foreigner, without a penny, it was quite clear that the elder Gibbon would never take her for a daughter-in-law. The famous 'sighed as a lover and obeyed as a son' sums up the situation so far as Gibbon was concerned. It must, I fear, be granted that Gibbon did not behave very prettily, and even leaves us with a vague impression that, if the paternal interdict had been wanting, some other obstacle would have turned up at the last moment. Modern readers will probably agree with Rous-

seau's judgment of the case.   Rousseau pitied
poor Susanne, but thought that Gibbon had shown
himself unworthy of her, and would only have
made her 'rich and miserable' in England.   As
Mlle. Curclod soon became Mme. Necker, and
forgave the lover who had jilted her, we may
forgive a misdoing which caused no permanent
misery.   This passing collocation of the two great
men, the sentimentalist who represents the passion,
and the calm, not to say cynical, historian who
represents the reflection of the period, is curiously
characteristic; and I leave the ethical question to
be settled by my readers.   Perhaps Gibbon was
not of the finest human clay; but the problem,
I repeat, was not how to make a perfect man, but
how to make a great historian.   Had Gibbon
become a husband there can be little doubt as
to the material consequences.   He had difficulties
enough in keeping up a bachelor establishment;
and with a wife by his side, he would have been
forced to accept an appointment—such as he
actually contemplated—in the Excise, and to
labour five days a week in official routine.   Julian
and Athanasius and Justinian must have waited
to be appreciated by somebody else.   The effect
upon Gibbon's character was exactly what was

wanted from the same point of view.   He made
up his mind soon afterwards, as appears from his
letters to his father, that he should never marry.
He was to be henceforth in that attitude of 'detachment' which constitutes the true historical
frame of mind—an interested looker-on, not an
active performer, in the great tragi-comedy.   It
may, perhaps, be suggested—with too much
plausibility—that the tone in which Gibbon
generally refers to love affairs in his history is not
altogether edifying, and hardly implies that his
passion had purified or ennobled his mind.   The
best arrangements will not work quite perfectly.
In any case, however, though Gibbon for sufficient
reasons treats the matter rather lightly, he had, as
he intimates, gone through one of the painful
crises which form epochs in the development of
character.   He was certainly not soured as some
men have been, but he henceforward cultivated
affections of a more tepid kind.   No man, it must
be always remembered, was a more thoroughly
faithful friend ; he showed very unusual gener-
osity and good-feeling to his father, his stepmother, and the aunt who had protected his
childhood.   It is impossible, for example, without
a very warm feeling of posthumous regard, to read

his letter to Lord Sheffield upon Lady Sheffield's death, and to remember how the gouty and preposterously fat old gentleman (old in constitution though not in years) bundled himself into his carriage, and set off to travel through the midst of armies to bring such solace to his friend as was possible. Meanwhile, he had been taught by a sharp enough lesson to know himself. He was not suited to come upon the stage as a Romeo, and must be content to play Horatio, a good, honest friend of more romantic and passionate characters. Henceforward it was to be his destiny to renounce the stronger impulses, and to devote himself in his little circle of friends to the great work for which so many forces within and without had been moulding him.

Before his love affair was over, Gibbon had been forced into experience of a different kind. He has told us himself how the captain of Hampshire grenadiers was of some use to the historian of the Roman Empire. Later critics have told us that, in fact, his narratives of military events show that he had profited by seeing a real flesh-and-blood army, on however small a scale, instead of only reading about armies in books. Of that I am an incompetent judge,

but on this and on his political career there is at
least an obvious remark to be made.   Gibbon
tells us himself how his service in the militia
made him an 'Englishman and a soldier,' and
how, in spite of all the waste of time, he still
travelled with a Horace 'always in his pocket and
often in his hand,' and, when the enforced fast
from literature came to an end, fell upon the old
feast with sharpened appetite, and rushed off as
rapidly as he could to find the inspiration for his
great book in Rome.   In other words, he was
brought into close contact with actual affairs, and
yet not diverted from the true aim of his life.
The political career had the same felicity.   He
found himself too slow and unready to speak, and
was content to be a quiet looker-on.   It must,
indeed, be admitted that he looked on with
superlative calmness.   His political career, says
Mr. Morison, is the 'side of his history from
which a friendly biographer would most readily
turn away.'   'I went into Parliament,' he says
himself, 'without patriotism and without ambi-
tion, and all my views tended to the convenient
and respectable place of a lord of trade.'   That,
certainly, is not an exalted view.   Moreover,
Gibbon's way of referring to contemporary events

shows apparent levity and even want of penetration.   He is less sagacious than Horace Walpole,
whose extraordinary cleverness was wasted by
frivolity.   As an outside observer, he might have
recognised the importance of the great issues, and
shown himself at least on a level with the higher
judges of his own time.   He was apparently
conscious of the gross blunders of George III.
and Lord North, but was content to support
Ministers, with a lazy indifference to the result.
His letters, when they contain any reference to
the American War, treat the matter almost as a
jest, and plainly betray that his real interest was
much more with Alaric than with Washington.
He lived through the most exciting period of
the century; he even took an actual, though a
very subordinate, part in the operations which
involved the foundation of the British Empire in
the East and the expulsion of our rivals from
the West.   He supported the political course
which led to the separation of our greatest
colonies a few years later ; and both at these'
periods and on the outbreak of the French
Revolution afterwards, he seems to have regarded
the greatest events of the time chiefly as they
affected the comfort of a fat historian in his

library. What defence can be made? None
truly, if we are measuring Gibbon by a lofty
moral standard; but if we are asking the
question now under consideration, how a great
historian was to be turned out, we shall have to
make a very different judgment.

The obvious reproach is summed up by the
statement that Gibbon was a cynic. The name
suggests the selfish indifference to human welfare
which permits a man to treat politics simply as a
game played for the stakes of place and pension.
It is generally added, though I hardly know
whether it is regarded by way of apology, or as
a proof of the offence, that all our great-grand-
fathers were corrupt borough-mongers, forming
cliques for the distribution of plunder, and caring
nothing for the welfare of the people. We
ought, we are often told, to judge a man by
the standard of his period. Whatever the period,
it can always be plausibly added that it was the
most immoral period ever known in history.
The argument is familiar, and I cannot attempt
to consider its precise application here. But I
may try briefly to indicate how it would have
struck Gibbon. What would he have said if he
could have foreseen the judgment of the coming

generation ?   You call me a cynic, he might have
replied, but at least you must admit that I was an
honest cynic ; I never professed to believe in
humbug, though I had to accept it.   If you
are less cynical, you have made up for it by
being more hypocritical.   Our party politics
meant adherence to some little aristocratic ring.
Yours mean servility to a caucus.   You cover a
real cynicism as deep as mine by shouting with
the largest mob.   We at least dared to despise
a demagogue ; you dare not openly deny his
inspiration.   You manage to use fine phrases
so as to cover the desertion of all your principles :
you use old war-cries in favour of the very
doctrines which you used to condemn, and
declare all the time that you are impelled by
' enthusiasm ' and sensibility to the voice of the
people.   Is it not rather subservience to their
narrowest prejudices ?   In my day, he would add,
we had examples of the genuine demagogue
revealing himself without a blush.   When in the
militia, in 1762, I saw Colonel Wilkes, the best
of companions, at a drunken dinner, full of
blasphemy and indecency, glorying in his
profligacy, and openly declaring that he had
resolved to make his fortune.   You have found

out that because he made it by flattering the
winning side he must have been a saint in
disguise.   You sneer at my want of ʻenthusiasm.'
You shudder when you make the remark that
enthusiasm was once actually a term of reproach.
When we denounced ʻenthusiasts,' we denounced
a very bad thing.   We thought that the false
claimants of supernatural powers must be knaves
or fools, and we ventured to say so openly.
You think that even a charlatan deserves respect
if his stock-in-trade is a comfortable superstition.
I, too, could claim enthusiasm in your sense.   It
was in a moment of ʻenthusiasm' that I joined
the Church of Rome ; and though I always scorned
to affect what I did not feel, it was with true
ʻenthusiasm' that I entered Rome, heard the
bare-footed friars singing vespers in the Temple
of Jupiter, and conceived the first crude idea of
my great work.   Enthusiasm, in my version,
lifted me to the regions of philosophy, and
separated me from the vulgar herd.   It did not
mean the discovery of the *vox dei* in every plat-
form intended to catch the votes of the majority.
We did not think ignorance and poverty a
sufficient guarantee for political or religious
infallibility.   But we were not, therefore, as you

infer, indifferent to the happiness of mankind.
We thought that their happiness was best secured
in the ages when a benevolent despotism main-
tained peace and order throughout the world;
when philosophers could rule and the lower
orders be confined to the work for which they
were really competent.   We held in religion
pretty much what you hold, only that you try
to cover your real meaning under a cloud of
words.   We accepted my great maxim : To the
philosopher all religions are equally false; and to
the magistrate equally useful.   You try to spin
theories which will combine the two opinions—
which will allow you to use the most edifying
language, while explaining that it means nothing;
and to base arguments for 'faith' on the admission that nobody can possibly know anything.
We were content to say that it was too much
honour to the vulgar to argue as to the truth of
their beliefs.   We were content to belong to the
upper circle of enlightenment in which it was
understood that the creeds were meaningless, but
without attempting the hopeless task of enlight-
ening the uncultivated mind.   Some such retort
might be made to the nineteenth century by the
eighteenth ; and Gibbon is a typical example of

the qualities which were denounced in the next generation when they called their immediate pre-decessors cold, heartless, and materialistic, and looked upon the whole preceding century as a sort of mysterious intercalation, an eclipse of all that was heroic and romantic, and a sudden paralysis of the progressive forces of humanity. Nothing, as I believe, can be more unjust; but rightly or wrongly, there are times when one regrets the reign of cool common sense and of freedom from fads and fussiness. At such moments there is an incidental charm about the intellectual position of our grandfathers. Philo-sophical problems can hardly be discussed now without suggesting some immediate practical application. Dogmas have become explosive, and suggest at once a reconstruction of society, a revolutionary or a reactionary movement; they are caught up by popular leaders on one side or the other, and abstract speculations are made at once into party watchwords. It must have been pleasant to philosophise in the days when your audience was select, when you could feel that your opinions would be discussed only by a few enlightened people, or would at most spread gradually and slowly force away old prejudices without provoking internecine struggles. You could boast of being a philosopher, and yet be content to allow error to die out among the vulgar without trying to force new ideas upon minds totally incapable of appreciating them. To speak freely and openly is no doubt the best rule in the long-run; but there is, it must be admitted, a real difficulty in proclaiming truth with the knowledge that it will be perverted by the vulgar inter-preters. To Gibbon, in his earlier days, that difficulty scarcely presented itself. He fancied that even his chapters upon Christianity would be accepted by all cultivated people, while there should be a faint understanding that the old language should still be kept up 'for the use of the poor.'

Gibbon, indeed, had in time to confess that this view involved an important practical mistake. Philosophy, political and religious, could not permanently remain the esoteric doctrine of a narrow circle; and when hot-headed Rousseaus and the like spread its tents among the vulgar, it produced an explosion which took the calm philosophers by surprise. Gibbon began to see a good side even in the superstition, the vitality of which had astonished him so much on the publication of his first volume.   This suggests the obvious weakness of his position ; nor do I mean to adopt the sentiments which I have ventured to attribute to him.   What I desire to indicate is the necessity of this position to the discharge of his function as a historian.   We can no doubt conceive of a more excellent way ; of a great thinker, who should at once be capable of philosophical detachment, of looking at passing events in their relations to the vast drama of human history on the largest scale without losing his interest in the history actually passing under his eyes.   He might take not less but more interest in processes which he saw to be the continuation of the great evolution of thought and society.   But the phrase indicates the conception which was necessarily obscure to Gibbon. To have reached that view would in his time have required almost superhuman attributes. Gibbon's merits were at the time inconsistent with the virtues of which we regret the absence. He had to choose, one may say, between two alternatives.   If he were to take an active part in the politics of the day, he would have had to be a Wilkes on condition of not being a Wilkeite, or at least, with Burke, to give up to party what was meant for mankind. To save him from such a fate, which would have been a hopeless waste of power, he required to be endowed with an excess of indifference, and a deficiency of close and spontaneous sympathy with men outside of his little inner circle. Of this, I fear, he cannot be acquitted. Indeed, his qualification in this respect went a little too far, for he appears to have been on the very point of accepting a post which would have cut short the *History* half-way. Even his best friends, strangely as it seems to us, pressed him to commit this semi-suicide. Here, therefore, his good genius had once more to interfere by external circumstances. The task was not difficult. A happy dulness to his claims was infused into the minds of the dispensers of patronage; and Gibbon was compelled to retire philosophically to the house at Lausanne, where in due time he was to take the famous stroll in the covered walk of acacias which on 27th June 1787 succeeded the completion of the 'last lines of the last page' of his unique achievement.

We see how strangely Gibbon had been fitted for his task; how fate had first turned him out of the quiet grooves down which he might have spun to obscurity, and then applied the goad judiciously whenever he tried to bolt from the predestined course.   The task itself was obviously demanded by the conditions of the time, and its importance recognised by other, and in some respects acuter or more powerful, intellects. History was to emerge from the stage of mere personal memoirs and antiquarian annals.   A survey from a higher point of view was wanted: a general map or panoramic view of the great field of human progress must be laid down as preparatory to further progress.   Such men as Hume and Voltaire, for instance, had clearly seen the need, and had endeavoured in their way to supply it.   Gibbon's superiority was, of course, due in the first place to the high standard of accuracy and research which has enabled his work to stand all the tests applied by later critics. His instinctive perception of this necessity, combined with the intellectual courage implied in his choice of so grand a subject, enabled him to combine width of view and fulness of detail with unsurpassed felicity.   All this is unanimously granted.   But other qualities were equally required, though from a later point of view they account rather for the limitations than the successes of his work.   There must be a division of labour between generations as well as between individuals.   Kepler had to describe the actual movements of the planets before Newton could determine the nature of the forces implied by the movements.   In Gibbon's generation it was necessary to describe the evolutions of the puppets which move across the stage of history.   His successors could then, and not till then, attempt to show what were the hidden strings that moved them.   Gibbon, it has been said, 'adheres to the obvious surface of events, with little attempt to place them beneath the deeper sky of social evolution.   He appreciates, it is suggested, neither the great spiritual forces nor the economic conditions which lie beneath the surface.   He calmly surveys the great stream of history, its mingling currents and deluges and regurgitations, the struggles of priests and warriors and legislators, without suggesting any adequate conceptions of what is called the social dynamics implied.   To him history appears to be simply a 'register of the crimes, follies, and misfortunes of mankind.'   The criticism, taking its truth for granted, amounts to saying that Gibbon had only gone as far as was in his time possible.   He must be philosopher enough to sympathise with the great intellectual movement of his time. Otherwise he could not have risen above the atmosphere of Oxford common-rooms, and could only have written annals or narratives on one side or the other of some forgotten apologetic thesis. But had the philosophic taste predominated, had his passions and his sympathies been more fervid, he must have fallen into the fallacies of his time. The enthusiastic or militant philosopher was, as I certainly think, doing an inestimable service in attacking superstition and bigotry.   But he was thereby disqualified as a writer not only of philosophical history, but even of such a record of facts as would serve for later historians.   Such a man as d'Alembert was inclined to wish that history in general could be wiped out of human memory. From the point of view characteristic of the eighteenth-century philosophers, history could be nothing but a record of the tyranny of kings and the imposture of priests.   Voltaire's *Essai sur les Mœurs* is delightful reading, but a caricature of history.   Gibbon might sympathise with this sentiment so far as to look with calm impartiality upon all forms of faith and government, but not so far as to pervert his *History* into a series of party pamphlets.   To him the American War, or the early democratic movements in England, were simply incidents in his great panorama : like the rise of the Christian Church, or the barbarian Moslems or the Crusades, they were eddies in the great confused gulf-stream of humanity. He could not believe in a sudden revelation of Reason, or the advent of a new millennium any more than in the second coming anticipated by the early Christians. To condemn his coldness may be right; but it is to condemn him for taking the only point of view from which his task could be achieved. He was philosopher enough to be impartial, not enough to be subject to the illusions, useful illusions possibly, of a sudden regeneration of mankind by philosophy. His political position was the necessary complement of his historical position. A later philosophy may have taught us how to see a process of evolution, a gradual working-out of great problems, even in the blind, instinctive aspirations and crude faiths of earlier ages. At Gibbon's time, he had to choose between rejecting them in the mass as mere encumbrances or renouncing them altogether. That is to admit that the one point of view which makes a reasonable estimate possible was practically excluded. On the other

hand, his historical instinct forced him at last
to set forth the material facts both impartially
and so grouped and related as to bring out the
great issues.   It is easy now both for positivists
and believers to show, for example, that his
account of the origins of Christianity was entirely
insufficient.   He explains, as has been remarked,
the success of the Church by the zeal of the early
disciples, and forgets to explain how they came
to be zealous.   Undoubtedly that is an omission
of importance.   What, however, Gibbon did was
not the less effectively to bring out the real
conditions of any satisfactory solution of the
greatest of historical problems.   Newman observed
how, in a later period, 'Athanasius stands out
more grandly in Gibbon than in the pages of
the orthodox ecclesiastical historians.'   That is
because he places all events in their true historical
setting.   In the writings of the apologists of the
time, the spread of Christianity was treated as
though converts had been made by producing
satisfactory evidence of miracles in a court of
justice.   Gibbon's famous chapters, however inadequate, showed at least that the development
of the new creed required for its expansion a
calm consideration of all the multitudinous forces

that go to building up a great ecclesiastical
hierarchy, and a testing by careful examination of
all the entries about saints and martyrs which
flowed so easily from the pens of enthusiastic
historians.   That his judgment should be final or
even coherent was impossible ; but it was an
essential step towards any such judgment as
could pass muster with a historian equipped with
the results of later thought and inquiry.

Upon this, however, it would be idle to say more.
I have only tried to point an obvious moral; to
show what a rare combination of circumstances
with character and intellect is required to produce
a really monumental work ; to show how easy it
generally is even for the competent man of genius
to mistake his path at starting or to be distracted
from it by tempting accidents ; how necessary
may be not only the intervention of fortunate
accidents, but even the presence of qualities
which, in other relations, must be regarded as
defects.   Happily for us, the man came when
he was wanted, and just such as he was wanted ;
but after studying his career, we understand better
than ever why great works are so rare.   We may
probably have known of men—many instances
might easily be suggested—who might be com-

pared to Gibbon in natural endowments, and who have left nothing but fragments, or been confined to obscure tasks, the value of which will never be sufficiently recognised.   It is only when the right player comes, and the right cards are judiciously dealt to him by fortune, that the great successes can be accomplished.

NOTE.—It may be worth while to explain Lord Sheffield's mode of constructing Gibbon's autobiography, as it is not explicitly set out in the recent publication.   Gibbon wrote six MSS., marked A to F.   A is confined to an account of previous Gibbons, and D is a brief account of his own life down to 1770.   Lord Sheffield only used these for the opening paragraphs.   Gibbon then wrote E, giving his life down to 1789; then C, a fuller redaction of E down to 1770; then B, a fuller redaction of C down to 1764; and finally F, a fuller redaction of B down to 1753.   Lord Sheffield follows the last version in each case, F to 1753, B from 1753 to 1764, C from 1764 to 1770, and E from 1770 to 1789.   He prefers the shorter account of the militia, however, in C to that in B; and restores a phrase or two dropped by Gibbon.   So the 'sighed as a lover and obeyed as a son,' and the description of Adam Smith as a 'master of moral and political wisdom' come from C.

ARTHUR YOUNG

THE name of Arthur Young suggests to most readers a discussion of the causes of the French Revolution. The importance of the famous *Travels in France* is in fact sufficiently shown by the frequent references of the most competent writers, both French and English. Mr. Morley, for example, declares that Young's evidence is of more value than all the speculations of Burke and Paine and Mackintosh—the English protagonists in the great controversy of the time. Young, again, had a great deal to say upon the state of Ireland in his day, besides being a leading authority upon the agricultural development of England. No one, however, need fear that this paper will lead him into profound economical, or political, or historical discussions. For the present purpose, I have rather to protest against a too probable inference suggested by these topics. Young's con-

188

nection with them may probably lead those who
know only his name to put him down summarily
in the great class bore ; to assume that he was only
a ponderous professor of the dismal science, or an
early example of that most estimable but not
always lively species, the highly intelligent poli-
tician who travels in vacation-time, storing his
mind with useful information to be radiated forth
in lectures and essays, and excite the admiration
of parliamentary constituencies. Young, no
doubt, deserves that kind of glory in a high
degree. What I wish to do is to call attention to
the fact that he was also a human being—or what
in our disagreeable modern slang is called a 'per-
sonality'—of great interest. He was not a
walking blue-book, but a highly sensitive, enthusiastic, impulsive, and affectionate man of flesh and
blood, whose acquaintance every sensible man
would have been glad to cultivate. His last
biographer congratulates the world upon the fact
that he did not, as he was tempted to do, become
a clergyman or a soldier. In either capacity his
peculiar talents would no doubt have been comparatively wasted. As a soldier, he would probably
have been known only by some ingenious but futile
enterprise. Had he taken orders he might have

rivalled the charm of some of his amiable contemporaries — Gilbert White of Selborne, for
example,—and would have been a model clergyman
of the good old patriarchal type ; but he would
hardly have made a mark upon theological speculation.   Yet his actual career, however appropriate
to his talent, was such as to draw a certain shade
over his personal qualities ; and as unfortunately
he was not commemorated at his death in an
adequate biography, they have, perhaps, not been
sufficiently recognised.   That a fuller recognition
is possible is due in great part to Miss Betham-
Edwards, who prefixed a short memoir to the last
edition of his *Travels in France* (1892).   Miss
Betham-Edwards did her duty excellently ; she
not only appreciates his qualities but had access to
unpublished sources, including diaries and letters
of great interest.   The necessary limits of a preface
prevented her from doing more than drawing a
sketch, life-like as far as it goes, which tantalises
the reader by brief glimpses of possible filling up
of details.   These details are partly supplied by
her more recent publication of Young's autobiography (1898).   Young was not a Gibbon, and
did not correct and rewrite four times over.   Miss

Betham-Edwards appears to have done her best by omitting superfluous digressions ; and in any case, has given us a life full of interesting indications of character.[1]

Arthur Young was born on 11th September 1741. He was the son of a respectable prebendary, who was chaplain to Speaker Onslow, and both squire and rector of the parish of Bradfield, near Bury St. Edmunds. His mother, whose maiden name was Cousmaker, was the descendant of a Dutchman who had followed William III. to England. Miss Betham-Edwards suggests that the pleasant rural district in which Young passed his infancy may account for his love of scenery. Something more would be required to explain whence a man, descended from Dutch and East

[1] Here and there the notes might be a little fuller, and some information might have been gleaned from a biographical dictionary. Thus, for example, the *Anti-Jacobin* mentioned at page 362 was not the famous journal edited by Gifford of the *Quarterly*, but its successor, a monthly magazine edited by a different Gifford. Readers might have been reminded that the ' Porcupine mentioned in the same place was the famous Cobbett, still in his unregenerate days, and supposed to be inspired by the Tories. Young himself appears to have confused the two Giffords. 'Peter Pindar' did so, when he, to his cost, tried to horsewhip W. Gifford for an attack really made in the magazine of John Gifford. This confusion constantly reappears, and may be just worth a warning word.

Anglian ancestry, derived the mercurial temperament which we do not generally associate with
either country.   Both father and mother, however,
were handsome and intelligent, and we do not
know enough of the laws of heredity to account
for the appearance of this brilliant contrast to the
ponderous squires of Suffolk and the three-breeched
merchants of Holland.   Anyhow, Arthur Young
showed his qualities early.   He learned little at his
school, Lavenham—partly, he thinks, because he
became so much a favourite with his teacher as
to be spared the usual discipline.   When he was
about ten, however, he was already ' writing a
history of England,' and at thirteen learning to
dance and falling in love with the beautiful daughter of a village grocer.   He was taken from school
at the age of sixteen and apprenticed to a mercan-
tile firm at King's Lynn.   There he again fell in
love, his first idol being the black-eyed daughter
of a partner in the firm, who was taking music-
lessons from Burney, then organist of Lynn, and
best known to most of us as Mme. d'Arblay's
father.   He was already writing pamphlets and
getting them published, receiving payment in
' books,' but apparently learned nothing of his
proper business.   At any rate, on his father's death

in 1759, he left Lynn, ' without education, profession, pursuits, or employment,' and for want of
other occupation, took a farm belonging to his
mother at Bradfield. To improve his prospects,
he married at the age of twenty-four (in 1765) a
Miss Martha Allen of Lynn, neither the first nor
second object of his adorations, which apparently
it would not be easy to enumerate. He might
have made a better choice. Mrs. Young is said to
have been shrewish, and Young certainly regretted
his precipitance. The marriage was unhappy from
the first ; and Young records that, even when his
wife was in good health, she became all the more
' irritable,' and life a mere ' scene of worrying.'
The lady was sister-in-law of Mrs. Stephen Allen,
Burney's second wife, and stepmother of Miss
Burney, who has left some characteristic touches.
Young confided to Miss Burney a few years later,
either from confidence in her prudence, she says,
or from his general ' carelessness of consequences,'
that he was the ' most miserable fellow breathing,'
and that 'if he were to begin the world again, no
earthly thing should prevail with him to marry.'
On the whole, one might expect that a youth, who
is bound to an uncongenial wife and proposes to
make his living by farming, chiefly because he

knows as little of any other employment as he does
of agriculture, has made an unpromising start in
life.   But those who may have made such a
prophecy had not taken into account Young's
marvellous elasticity.   He was one of the men
who, if in the depths of depression at one moment,
are sure to be at the height of exhilaration in the
next.   Nothing could permanently suppress or
daunt him.   Compensations were sure to turn up.
If his wife was for the most part a thorn in his
flesh, he was at least a most affectionate father.
His own farming operations were as little successful
as though his lot had been cast in the worst days of
depression; but they entitled him to set up almost
at once as an authority upon the theory of agriculture.   He made tours, and published accounts of
his observations.   The result of his own experience
was, as he puts it, 'nothing but ignorance, folly,
presumption, and rascality' (the rascality, we hope,
in spite of the grammar, was that of his neighbours);
but he learned to judge of other people's farms,
and his books were of most singular 'utility to the
general agriculture of the kingdom.'   He failed at
his native place, after a short time, and immediately
took a larger farm, and had to pay £100 to
another man to take it off his hands, when his

successor made a fortune out of it. At a third farm
he spent nine years, with the sensation of having
been all the time 'in the jaws of a wolf.'[1] He
had, he says, tried 3000 experiments ; and must
therefore be reckoned wise if we may invert
Darwin's criterion that a fool is a man who never
tried an experiment. There is, however, such a
thing as being wise for others instead of for oneself. Whether Young's general views were sound
is more than I know. They were at least stimulating. He was becoming well known to agricultural reformers, and from 1773 to 1776 he
travelled in Ireland, where he was, for a short time,
agent to Lord Kingsborough's estates in County
Cork. Whatever was the result to Lord Kingsborough, Young's experience was embodied in a
book upon Ireland second only in value to the
French travels. He settled again at Bradfield
upon his mother's property, and there, after a time,
started a new project. Next to the farming without experience, one of the most promising roads to
ruin that can be suggested is starting a serious
and scientific periodical. Young accordingly in
1738 set up the *Annals of Agriculture*, which was

---

[1] See also Young's statement in *Annals of Agriculture*, vol. xv.

to be the organ of all benevolent men and good farmers. It certainly succeeded in so far as it attracted notice ; and it is worth turning over, not only for Young's own articles, but because it contains contributions from many of the most distinguished men of the time upon important topics. The poor-laws, for example, are discussed by Jeremy Bentham and Sir F. Eden, the author of the leading book upon the subject. Another contributor, who conceals himself under the modest name of ' Ralph Robinson, farmer at Windsor,' was no less a person, as Young tells us, than George III. himself.[1] Young, however, has still to complain of his financial results. His circulation only amounts after seven years to 350 ; and he is still engaged in the familiar employment of flogging a dead horse. The *Annals* only just paid their way ; but they spread his fame. His name on the title-page is followed by a list of titles which shows that he had received honours in France, Russia, Germany, Italy, and Switzerland. Among his admirers was the phil-

---

[1] George III. was believed by Bentham to have been his anonymous antagonist in a newspaper controversy, and to this circumstance the philosopher attributed the king's lasting antipathy to the famous ' Panopticon.' Bentham, I guess, was the victim of a practical joke in this instance; but Young appears to speak from knowledge.— *Autobiography*, p. 112.

anthropic Duke de Liancourt—the Anglomaniac
French nobleman who announced to Louis xvi.
that the fall of the Bastile was not a revolt but
a revolution. On Liancourt's invitation Young
made his famous French tours from 1787 to 1790.

The travels are most deservedly famous, but
they have hardly been popular in the same pro-
portion. In French, indeed, they have had a very
large circulation ; but in England they brought
more fame than profit. They owe such popularity as they achieved to the advice of a very
sensible friend. The tour in Ireland, said this
adviser, had no great success, because it was chiefly
a 'farming diary.' It was filled with elaborate
statistics and tables of prices which presupposed
a strong appetite for information in the reader.
The right plan to gain readers was to put down
the notes made at the moment as they occurred to
him. The book might lose in solidity, but would
gain in vivacity. Young fortunately took this
advice, which deserves to be recorded as one of the
few known instances of advice by which an author
has actually profited. It was, in fact, singularly
appropriate, for Young was essentially a man
whose first impressions were the most valuable,
as well as the most amusing. It is often better to

know what a man thought than to know what he afterwards thought that he ought to have thought. 'I was totally mistaken in my prediction,' as he quaintly remarks in a note to his *Travels*, 'and yet, on a revision, I think that I was right in it.' That is, the facts which really happened were those which, at the time, were the most unlikely to happen. Few historical facts, indeed, are more interesting than the visions, never to be precisely realised, which animated the imagination of the first observers of great movements. Young, too, was better at observation than at reflection. When he revised his journals of former tours and cut out the personal elements, he was substituting a set of statistical diagrams for a concrete picture ; and he filled the vacant space by economic speculations often of very inferior merit. Miss Betham-Edwards, indeed, declares, as it is natural for an enthusiastic biographer to declare, that Young instinctively anticipated Adam Smith, and Mill, and Cobden, and all the pundits of political economy. He was, if I may be pardoned for saying so, much too charming a person to deserve that equivocal praise. He is delightful by reason of his vivacity, his amiable petulance, and unconscious inconsistencies. The wisest philosopher, if

he honestly put down his first thoughts, would
be always contradicting himself. We get the
appearance of consistency only because we take
time to correct, and qualify, and compare, and
extenuate, and very often we spoil our best
thoughts in the process. What would not Mr.
Ruskin lose if he cared for consistency? The
price of suppressing first thoughts may be worth
paying by a man whose strength lies in logic;
but with a keen, rapid, impetuous observer like
Arthur Young we would rather do the correct-
ing for ourselves. His best phrases are im-
promptu ejaculations. 'Oh, if I were Legislator
of France for a day,' he exclaims, at the sight of
estates left waste for game-preserving, 'I would
make such great lords skip again!' These sentiments, he assures the reader, were 'those of the
moment,' and he was half inclined to strike out
many such passages. It was because they were
'of the moment' that they are so impressive.
Had he omitted them he would have taken off
the edge of his best passages, though he might
have expressed his later views more correctly.

This temperament, I need hardly argue, is not
the ideal one for a political economist. His
views should be expressible in columns of figures,

and he should never let a vivid impression guide him till he has reduced it to tangible statements of loss and gain. He must deal in sober black and white, and be on his guard against the brilliant shifting colours which are apt to generate illusions as to the real proportions of the objects of vision. Young, indeed, was a sound economist, and that, no doubt, is what Miss Betham-Edwards means, in so far as he was a thorough Free-Trader.   The 'whole system of monopoly,' he declares, 'is rotten to the core, and the true principle and vital spring and animating soul of commerce is LIBERTY!'   That, however sound may be the doctrine, is the utterance of an enthusiast, not of a sober, logical reasoner. He was animated by the spirit of the contemporary philosophy. The great object of his idolatry was Rousseau. In his French travels he visits the tomb of that 'immortal' and 'splendid genius' whose 'magic' is teaching French mothers to nurse their children, and French nobles to love a country life. He denounces the 'vile spirit of bigotry' which hunted Rousseau during his life as though he had been a mad dog.   At Chambery he turns even from his economical speculation to something still more interesting, the house of the 'deliciously amiable'

Mme. de Warens, and described 'by the inimitable pencil of Rousseau.' He sought for information about the lady, and could only discover that she was 'certainly dead.' In fact, as he produces a certificate of the occurrence of that event some thirty years before, there seems to be no reason for doubting it. With this enthusiasm Young found a keen interest in the writings of the French economists, whose theory of the surpassing importance of agriculture was more congenial to him than Adam Smith's rival doctrines. One of the most amusing episodes in his French travels records his visit to the scene of the labours of the great Marquis de Turbilly. The reader who is ashamed of not remembering the name may be comforted by finding that even in his own country the great man's memory had faded within twelve years of his death. Young, however, boldly introduced himself to the new proprietor of the estates, was introduced to one of Turbilly's old labourers, and went off happy with an autograph of the great marquis to be placed among his curiosities. Other pilgrimages of the same kind, to places connected with names faintly remembered, it is to be feared, in England, prove the keenness of Young's interest in the literature

of his favourite subject.   Young's belief in Free
Trade implies his acceptance of the chief doctrine
of the Economists, and his sympathy with the
general movement of the time.   Any one who
should be surprised that Young as the staunchest
of agriculturists was not a Protectionist would,
of course, be guilty of an anachronism.   In those
days Adam Smith observes that the landowning
classes are far more liberal than the manufacturers.
England was only just ceasing to export corn,
and Young was roused to his most indignant
mood by the desire of the clothmakers to maintain restrictions upon the exports of English
wool.   What he really illustrates, indeed, is the
spirit which we generally associate with the great
revolution of manufactures, as applied to the
contemporary development of agriculture.

Another variety of Young's enthusiasm makes
a pleasant and characteristic contrast to his discussions as to the prices of corn and rates of
wages.   A genuine love of scenery breaks out
in his English tours, though it is generally con-
signed to the notes, the text being preserved for
the graver purposes of statistical information.   It
has, too, a peculiar turn which marks the man.
It may be doubted whether our admiration for

'Nature' is really so new as we sometimes fancy.
The old squire or country parson may have loved
the forest or the moor as well as his descendants,
though his love was unconscious. The scenery
may have given a charm to his favourite pursuits,
his fishing or his hunting, though he did not talk
about it, or even know it. Scenery, even in
poetry, was kept in the background of human
figures, but was not less distinctly present. In
Young's time, however, the country gentleman
was becoming civilised and polished; he was
building mansions with classical porticoes, filling
them with pictures bought on the 'grand tour,'
and laying out grounds with the help of Kent or
a 'capability' Brown. He was beginning, that
is, to appreciate the advantage of adapting the
environment to his dwelling-place; and the new
art of 'landscape gardening' was putting the old
formal gardens out of fashion. Pope's garden at
Twickenham had become famous, and Shenstone,
as Johnson puts it, had 'begun to point his
prospects, to diversify his surface, to entangle his
walks, and to wind his waters; which he did with
such judgment and such fancy, as made his little
domain the envy of the great and the admiration
of the skilful.' Johnson will not inquire whether

this ' demands any great powers of mind,' but he
admits that ' to embellish the form of nature is an
innocent amusement.' Young, who was a most
determined and indefatigable sightseer, had no
misgivings about the 'powers of mind' required.
He visits the houses of the nobility most conscientiously, gives little criticisms of their pictures,
which have at least the merit of perfect simplicity,
and falls into ecstasies over the 'embellishments
of the form of nature.' He visited the Lakes
at the time when Gray was writing his now
celebrated letters, and his descriptions are equally
enthusiastic, if not of equal literary excellence.
He 'does' the neighbourhood of Keswick in the
most systematic way ; and, I am glad to say it to
his honour, is not content without climbing to the
top of Skiddaw. He complains gently, however,
that art has not been properly called in to the aid
of nature. He would like winding walks and
properly-fenced seats, which should enable him
to look comfortably from the edge of precipices,
and be led to them as a well-arranged surprise.
His eloquence is stimulated to the highest flights
when he visits Persfield on the 'Why' (as he
spells the river's name). There a judicious im-
prover has laid out an estate in the most skilful

way, so as to display the glories of the Wyndcliff
and its neighbourhood. Young is almost carried
off his feet by his delight, but he recovers sufficiently to intimate some gentle and apologetic
criticisms. He gives us an æsthetic discussion as
to the correct method of mixing the sublime with
the beautiful in due proportions. Young's contemporary, Gilpin, remarks of the same place that
it is not ' picturesque,' but extremely romantic,
and gives a loose to the ' most pleasing riot of the
imagination.' Nothing in the way of literature
seems to keep so ill as æsthetic criticism ; and we
must not be hard upon these poor old gentlemen.
They held that nature wanted a little judicious
arranging and dramatising. At Wentworth he
pronounces that the woods and waters are
' sketched with great taste,' and that the woods
in particular have a ' solemn brownness' which is
gratifying to the connoisseur. Young had not
read Wordsworth, for obvious reasons, and when
he wants a bit of poetry has generally to resort
to Pope's ' breathes a browner horror o'er the
woods.' He much approves of a statue of Ceres
and ' a Chinese temple' which temper the rawness
of nature at Wentworth ; and elsewhere he gives
another of his artless æsthetic disquisitions upon

the proper theory of sham ruins. They ought, he thinks, to represent the real thing, and should not be made into mere places for tea-drinking. Whatever may be Young's limitations, however, it is impossible to doubt that his enthusiasm for the beauties of nature is as hearty and genuine as that of Gray or of any of the generation which learned its canons of taste from Wordsworth. At Killarney, for example, he is thrown into raptures of the most orthodox variety, and when he comes within sight of the Pyrenees Mr. Ruskin himself could not accuse him of deficient feeling. ' This prospect' (from Montauban), he says, 'which contains a semicircle of a hundred miles in diameter, has an oceanic vastness in which the eye loses itself; an almost boundless scene of cultivation; an animated, but confused, mass of infinitely varied parts, melting gradually into the distant obscure, from which emerges the amazing frame of the Pyrenees, rearing their silvered heads far above the clouds.' Young, one cannot doubt after reading this and other passages, would have been in these days an honorary member of the Alpine Club, as well as of his numerous foreign agricultural societies.

There is, indeed, one exception to his enthu-

siasm. He would not have accepted Scott's love
of the heather. He always speaks of 'heather
and ling' with a kind of personal animosity.
They are signs of the abomination of desolation.
His criticism of French chateaux shows both
sentiments. He is shocked, and with sufficient
reason, at the game-preserving wastes which sur-
round them ; but he is also disgusted, in a minor
degree, by the want of proper landscape-garden-
ing. Their great houses are often built in the
purlieus of a town ; and what might be made
into beautiful grounds abandoned to the baser
purposes of stables or other utilitarian erections.
Young naturally has the eye of the country
gentleman, as his successor Cobbett had the eye
of the practical farmer. Neither could take the
simply sentimental view ; and in each, therefore,
a most genuine love of country scenery is combined with an almost fanatical horror of a waste.
Young would have sympathised with Cobbett's
denunciation of the 'accursed hill' of Hindhead,
which some of us now find to possess certain
charms ; or have approved Defoe's remark, that
Bagshot Heath had been placed by Providence so
near to London in order to rebuke the pride of
Englishmen by showing that the heart of their

own country could be as desolate as a Scottish moor. Young, however, approved what Cobbett has begun to dread, the application to agriculture of the same spirit which was creating the manufacturing system. His ideal was the improving landlord. He accepts Gulliver's maxim that the man who could make two blades of grass grow where one had grown before, could deserve more of his country than all the politicians put together. Young had, as he said, passed his life up to fifty in trying to fulfil that duty; and he was not less energetic afterwards. It sums up his whole code of conduct. Every political and economical project was to be estimated by its tendency to increase the produce of agriculture. Other ends are secondary. The sight of land which might bear corn and only produced ling vexes his very soul. He regarded Enfield Chase as a simple ' nuisance '—a scandal to the Government of the country,—and he calculates that Salisbury Plain might be made to grow food for the whole population. For sympathy, again, he looked to the country gentleman. Not one farmer in five thousand, he complains, ever read a book; he is not foolish enough to waste his missionary zeal upon them; but the country happily abounds

with gentlemen-farmers, and they are the sources
of all improvement. His heroes are Tull, who
introduced turnips; and Weston, who introduced
clover; and Lord Townshend and Mr. Allen,
who introduced marling into Norfolk. Wher-
ever he sees a gentleman who has the sense to
devote himself to such labours, he pours out
blessings on his head. I do not know whether
he is most enthusiastic over the Marquis of
Rockingham, who had taught the farmers of
Yorkshire to grow better crops; or over the
Duke of Bridgewater, whose great canal was
among the first symptoms of the great manufacturing development of Lancashire. He has
an incarnation of the spirit of improvement
which was transforming England in his days;
and there is something pleasant in his sanguine
optimism as to public affairs, when his own little
enterprises were anything but prosperous. The
darker side of the great industrial revolution
which was to alarm Cobbett was still hidden
from him. The growth of pauperism, which
began with war and famine at the end of the
century, was still in the future. In the earlier
period all patriots were still lamenting over an
imaginary decline of the population, which could

not be disproved by the imperfect statistics of the time. Young has to meet their jeremiads by rather conjectural figures, as well as by his own observations of growing prosperity on all sides. His views are often oddly different from those which came up with the next generation. He denounces the poor-laws partly on the familiar ground that they are demoralising incentives to idleness. But he hates them still more because they were, as he puts it, 'framed in the very spirit of depopulation.' He reckons it as one of the great advantages of Ireland that the absence of poor-laws encourages a rapid increase of the numbers of the people. No one could speak more warmly of the importance of improving the condition of the poor in Ireland and else-where, but he has no thought of the dangers which alarmed Malthus and the later economists. The one merit of the old poor-laws according to them was that the parishes had an interest in checking the growth of the population. That, according to Young, was the cardinal vice of the system. The great aim of the statesman should be an increase of population. The way to increase population is to take all fetters from industry. Cultivate waste lands; turn Salisbury

Plain into arable fields; carry cultivation, as
Macaulay hoped we should do, to the top of
Helvellyn and Ben Nevis; make roads and
canals; introduce threshing-machines and steam-
engines, and population will increase with the
means of employment. He is a little puzzled at
times by the conflict of interests. Low wages,
he remarks, are good for the employer; and he
observes that, in London, wages are high.
Therefore, he argues, the statesman should limit
the size of London. There are other reasons for
this. London is a devouring gulf; the deaths
greatly exceed the births; it is actually eating
away population, and should somehow be kept
down in the interests of agriculture. Another
symptom which vexes Young's soul is the
enormous consumption of tea. Tea, in the first
place, is debilitating generally, and therefore tends
to diminish numbers; and, in the second place,
it is unfavourable to agriculture. If all the
money spent upon tea were spent upon corn,
enough corn could be raised, as he calculates, to
support four millions of people. Finally, the
money spent upon tea is all thrown away upon
the Chinese instead of supporting British industry. He is following the lead of Jonas Hanway,

whose arguments to the same effect had provoked Johnson's famous eulogy upon his favourite
beverage.   Young was evidently rather vague in
his political economy; though it would be unfair
to take some of these *obiter dicta*, thrown out on
the spur of the moment, as his definite conclusions.   In another respect, Young is very unlike
his followers.   How are we to get rich? he asks;
and his answer is, by increasing our debt of 140
millions to 200 millions.   The additional sum,
he explains, is to be spent on reclaiming waste
lands.   He wishes Government to interfere ener-
getically, and complains bitterly that English
statesmen   have   always   neglected   agriculture.
England, as he tells a French friend, 'has had
many Colberts but not one Sully.'   Our hus-
bandry has flourished in the teeth of our
Ministers, and is far from what it would be
had it received the same attention as trade and
manufactures.   Once more, to make two blades
grow in the place of one is the ultimate object
of all rational conduct, the tendency to produce
that result the criterion of all policy, and energy
in bringing it about the duty of all ministers,
politicians, and private persons.   All good things
will follow.

Young's devoted and unflagging zeal, and his sanguine confidence in his principles is equally attractive, whatever the inconsistencies or rashness of his speculations. This must be remembered in reading his French travels. Young is generally cited as justifying the Revolution, and his later recantation regarded as one of the many instances of inconsistency due to the Reign of Terror. It must be observed, however, and it certainly does not diminish the value of his evidence, that Young was never a thorough political follower of the revolutionists. His real sympathy was with his Anglomaniac friends, Liancourt and his like. The question is, as he says in 1789, whether the French will adopt the British Constitution with improvements, or listen to speculative theorists. The result in the latter case would be 'inextricable confusion and civil wars.' Young's great merit is precisely that he records his impressions of fact so vividly and candidly that the value of his evidence is quite independent of the correctness of his political conclusions. I will not ask what those conclusions should be. Young's point of view is the characteristic point for us. The French conditions inverted his English experience. In England he has to be constantly lamenting the want of roads ; but what roads there were were thronged.   In France there are magnificent roads, but 'circulation is stagnant.'   In Languedoc he passes ' an incredible number of splendid bridges and many superb causeways,' but a certain *Croix Blanche* is an ' execrable receptacle of filth, vermin, impudence, and imposition,' presided over by ' a withered hag, the demon of beastliness.'   Not a carriage is to be had.   In England you have towns of 3000 people cut off from all high-roads, yet with clean inns, civil hosts, and a postchaise ready at a moment's notice.   Young wishes to have both the energetic Government and the energy of private enterprise.   He admires the great public works of France, but is stirred to wrath by the apathy of the individual Frenchman. Though he is constantly acknowledging the courtesy of Frenchmen, and their superiority in many points of refinement, he is oddly annoyed by their taciturnity.   He can never get any adequate conversation at a *table d'hote*.   Possibly the excellent Young, who was clearly ready to talk to anybody, was a little impeded in France by the fact that (as we learn from Miss Burney) his knowledge of the language was limited, and he filled up any gaps by inserting English words

with an imitation of the French accent. He
could certainly make a speech under pressure, for
he describes how he once pacified a suspicious
mob, which thought that the inquisitive traveller
must be devising schemes for taxation. He
pointed out that in his own country the rich
were taxed for the poor,—there was some good in
the poor-laws, after all! But a further explana-
tion is suggested by his lamentation over the
surprising ignorance of their own affairs in the
provinces. There were no newspapers and no
political talk, even at the exciting times of the
Revolution. Petty English tradesmen, he declares,
were talking about the last news from France all
over the country, before any interest in the
matter had spread to the people directly affected.
In English counties the newspaper circulated from
the squire's hall to the farmer or the small artisan;
but the French *seigneurs* formed no centres of
superior enlightenment. They crowded into the
towns and spent their rents upon the theatres;
they only visited the country when they were
banished; and then they turned great districts
into mere wildernesses to be roamed over by
boars, wolves, and deer. They made one blade
grow where two had grown before. Young

admired the English country gentleman as the active supporter and originator of all improvements. His French rival was a mere incubus, an effete 'survival.' In France, according to Young, half, if not two-thirds of the land was already in the hands of small proprietors. Peasants supplied the industry, and carried out what improvements there were. They illustrated his famous phrase, 'The magic of property turns sand to gold.' Meanwhile the great *seigneurs* do nothing; they receive quit-rents and enforce *tailles* and *corvées*, and all the oppressive incidents of feudal tenure. Young accordingly transfers to the peasantry the sympathy which in England he felt for the country gentleman. He did not object to the large proprietor as such; but to the proprietor, large or small, who did not do his duty by his property. He draws up an indictment against the French nobility, which is all the more impressive because it does not imply any preconceived political theories. At one moment he even approves of the French peasantry for seizing waste lands by force, and even wishes that the English peasantry were authorised to take similar steps. After all, waste land is the great evil of the world. But it is quite intelligible that from his point of view the actual course of affairs in France should have convinced him that too high a price might be paid even for the appropriation of a waste. In England, Young's zeal for agricultural improvements was never qualified. It must, he was clear, be good for everybody. He tells land-lords that they are foolish for boasting of not raising their rents. To raise rents (within limits, he admits) is the best way of stimulating industry. His ideal person is a certain wonderful collier. The owner of the property had tried to improve the condition of his workmen by giving them small allotments of waste land. One of them worked from midnight till noon in the mine, and after his twelve hours spent eight more upon im-proving his bit of land, removing gigantic stones, and finally turning nine or ten acres into cultivated fields. Young celebrates this extraordinary feat of labouring twenty hours a day for several years with characteristic enthusiasm, and offers to receive subscriptions for the hero, which, we will hope, enabled the poor man to be less industrious.

At a splenetic moment during his French travels, Young, riding on a blind mare, just misses a meeting with Charles Fox, who had excited the wonder of the natives by his modesty

in travelling with nothing but a postchaise, a
cabriolet for his servants, and a courier to order
horses. ' A plague on a blind mare ! ' exclaims
Young ; ' but I have worked through life, and he
(that is, Fox) TALKS ! ' Young had talked a good
deal too, especially on paper ; but his momentary
grumble was pardonable. His ' 3000 experiments,'
and his various attempts to get out of perpetual
anxiety had brought him little but reputation.
George III., indeed, sent him a merino ram, much
to his satisfaction ; it proved that the king had
just views of glory, and that a period was coming
when ' more homage' would be paid to a prince
for giving ' a ram to a farmer than for wielding
a sceptre.' George III. soon found it necessary to
devote more time to his sceptre than to his rams ;
but Young's career was more affected, happily or
otherwise, by another influence. Sir John Sinclair
was an ideal representative of the dismal science.
He atoned for being an intolerable bore by doing
some excellent work. He inherited a large estate
in Caithness, and began his reign by assembling
his tenants and making in one day a road over an
inaccessible hill ; and he set to work enclosing,
rearranging farms, introducing fisheries, and
generally rousing the primitive Gaelic population
to a sense of the advantages of civilisation. He

promoted agricultural societies, and introduced
the 'long sheep' into the Highlands. His son
tells us that due regard was paid in his improvements to the interests of the poor ; that a tide of
prosperity set in, and population increased rapidly.
At any rate, Sinclair translated into practice
Young's most cherished principles. Sinclair sat
at the feet of Adam Smith ; and travelled to
Sweden and Russia in search of information ; and
wrote a *History of the Revenue* ; and became a
Member of Parliament. He began, in 1791, to
publish a book of great value, the *Statistical
Account of Scotland.* He is said to have been the
first person to introduce the word 'statistical' into
English ; and this book, a collection of reports
from the ministers of all the Scottish parishes,
was of great importance at a time when people
did not even know for certain whether population
was increasing or declining. Sinclair, in 1793,
persuaded Pitt to start the 'Board of Agriculture.'
Arthur Young had bet the nineteen volumes of
his *Annals* against the twenty-one of Sinclair's
Statistical Account that Pitt would not consent.[1]
He lost the bet, to his great satisfaction; for,
though the Minister would only allow £3000 a

[1] A brief and interesting *History of the Board of Agriculture* has just
been published by Sir Ernest Clarke, secretary to the Royal Agricultural Society.

year, Young was made secretary with a salary of £400. Now, with the help of Sinclair, he could set to work and, on however modest a scale, Government would at last set about producing those two blades of grass. Their first aim was to do in England what Sinclair had done in Scotland. The English clergy were to be asked to rival the Scottish ministers. But here occurred a significant difficulty. One of Young's pet theories was that tithes were an intolerable burthen to agriculture. He would not confiscate them, but would commute them for an increase of glebe. The English clergy, he explains, had so little to do that they naturally took to dancing and sporting, if not to still less decorous pursuits. Agriculture was the natural employment for them, as, indeed, it was the ideal occupation for every one. The clergy, however, suspected, not unnaturally, that gentlemen of these views might be insidiously attacking the tithes, and would probably be putting awkward questions. The Archbishop of Canterbury protested; and the Board had to be less inquisitive, and confined itself in this direction to publishing a number of reports upon the agriculture of counties. They tried, however, to promote their grand object by other means. The worthy

Sinclair once made a joke—not, it is true, of the
first water ; but still, as it was his only joke, he
naturally repeated it as often as possible. This
was to give as a toast, 'May commons become
uncommon!' He fully shared Young's mania.
What is the use, he would inquire, of conquering
colonies? Let us first conquer Finchley Common,
and compel Epping Forest to 'submit to the yoke
of improvement.' His son claims for him the
merit of actually making the suggestion which led
to the enclosure of Hounslow Heath. With all
their energy, Sinclair and Young could never
persuade Parliament to pass a General Enclosure
Bill ; but they claimed to have facilitated the
process which went on so rapidly in their time.
The common field system, the source of all
slovenly agriculture according to him, was very
rapidly broken up. Meanwhile, it is to be feared,
the Board became rather a nuisance. It was a
rather anomalous body, with no very definite
functions ; and it went about like an intrusive
busybody, trying to stir up people in general by
every means in its power. It offered premiums
for inventions, and encouraged scientific writers
to give lectures and produce books, and held
meetings where good agriculturists might make

each other's acquaintance; but it is said to have ultimately become a kind of political debating society, and finally expired (1822) two years after Young's death.   In spite of their agreement upon the main point, Young soon found the chief of the new board to be far from congenial.   Sinclair was a pushing, self-seeking person, stingy in money matters, industrious in the wrong direction, and as anxious to establish his own claims as to promote the true interests of agriculture.   Young was relieved when for a time Sinclair was superseded.   He returned to be tried, however, 'under promises of good behaviour,' at a time (1805) when Young was threatened with blindness and falling into melancholy.

Sinclair about 1810 returned to Scotland, where he got a good appointment and leisure for liberally bestowing his tediousness upon his countrymen and the world.   He got up Highland games; promoted the use of the bagpipes, and defended the authenticity of Ossian.   He gave advice to Scott in literary matters.   He expounded his opinions in numerous pamphlets—his son gives a list of 367 of these productions,—and, finding the employment insufficient, spent his spare time in composing four gigantic cyclopædias, which were to codify all human knowledge upon health, agriculture, religion, and political economy. The first two alone were published, and I confess that I have not read nor even seen them. It appears, however, from *The Edinburgh Review* (October 1807) that the first fills four volumes of 800 closely printed pages apiece; marked, as the reviewer asserts, in the good old style, by 'indistinctness,' 'incredible credulity,' 'mawkish morality,' 'marvellous ignorance,' and a 'display of the most diffuse, clumsy, and superficial reasoning.' The reviewer gives as specimens Sinclair's remarks upon the advantage of taking butter with fish; and his proof that, although the stomach is an organ not remarkable for external elegance, it not the less requires careful attention in consequence of its delicate structure. Sinclair probably opposed a good solid stolidity to this heartless levity. He proposed that his work should be translated into the principal languages of Europe, and promised that it should add from ten to thirty years to the life of every attentive reader. Apparently he had the reward appropriate to gentle dulness, for it is said that five editions were sold—a sufficient answer to any review. Sinclair survived till 1835.

Meanwhile Arthur Young had a more pathetic end. His secretaryship had taken him to London. there his handsome presence and open-hearted, cordial ways made him acceptable in society, which he heartily enjoyed. But his life was cruelly darkened. He was tenderly attached to his youngest daughter 'Bobbin,' to whom, in her infancy, he wrote pleasant little letters, and whom he never forgot in his travels. 'I have more pleasure,' he says at the end of his first tour in France, 'in giving my little girl a French doll than in viewing Versailles,' and 'viewing Versailles' was no small pleasure to him. Her death in 1797 struck a blow after which he never quite recovered his cheerfulness. His friends thought that a blindness which soon followed was due to 'excess of weeping.' I do not know whether physicians would regard this as a possible cause of cataract. An operation for this disease was performed eleven years later, and recovery promised on condition of calmness. Wilberforce, coming to see him, told him of the death of the Duke of Grafton, now chiefly remembered by the abuse of Junius. The duke, however, became serious in his later years, and was one of Young's improving landlords. Anyhow, the news, or

Wilberforce's comments, provoked a burst of tears which was fatal to Young's hopes of recovery. He retired to his native village, and sought for consolation in religious practices. He had upon the loss of his daughter studied religious books for sixteen or seventeen hours a day, and had been profoundly affected by Wilberforce's *Practical View of Christianity*. As he was forced to retire from business, he became a more zealous disciple, and tried to propagate his faith. He published little selections from the works of Baxter and Owen, and preached on Sunday evenings in a hall at Bradfield. 'There is still living (1889) a nonagenarian at Bradfield,' writes Miss Betham, 'who remembers his sermons.' The blind old man 'would get his back turned to his audience, and have to be put straight by his daughter and secretary.' He still worked at his favourite pursuit, and left ten folio volumes in manuscript of a History of Agriculture. He died 20th April 1820. The nonagenarian of 1889 is by this time, if he survives, probably a centenarian; but it is curious to reflect that we have still among us men of active minds whose careers overlap Young's. His enthusiasm refers to a strangely altered state of things. What he would think of the present state of England, of modern London, of the imports of tea, of the growth of population, and of agricultural depression, it is needless to conjecture. No doubt he would admit that some of his predictions have turned out badly, but he would perhaps hold not the less that he was right in making them. The short-sightedness of the most intelligent observers suggests comfort when one studies some modern prophets.

WORDSWORTH'S YOUTH [1]

A FRENCH critic, M. Émile Legouis, has written a singularly interesting study of Wordsworth's youth. Of M. Legouis's general qualifications, it need only be said that he has a thorough knowledge of English literature, and a minute acquaintance with all the special literature bearing upon Wordsworth's early career. He fully appreciates the qualities which, though they have endeared Wordsworth's poetry to his own countrymen, have hardly made him one of the cosmopolitan poets. I do not, however, propose to say anything of Wordsworth's general merits. M. Legouis's study is concerned with one stage in Wordsworth's development. Wordsworth was in France at the crisis of the Revolution, and there, as we know from the *Prelude,* became the enthusiastic admirer of Michel Beaupuy, afterwards a general and an incarnation of republican

---

[1] *La Jeunesse de Wordsworth.* Par Émile Legouis. Paris, 1896. An English translation appeared in 1897.

virtue. Wordsworth compares him to Dion as the philosophic assailant of a tyrant.[1] M. Legouis has already given an account of Beaupuy,[2] and has now pointed out the nature of his influence upon his young English disciple.

Browning's *Lost Leader* represented a view of Wordsworth which seemed strange to most readers. The name of Wordsworth had come to suggest belief in the Thirty-nine Articles, capital punishment, and rotten boroughs. Some of us can still remember the venerable grey head bowed in the little church at Grasmere, and typifying complete acquiescence in orthodox tradition. This ' lost leader,' however, had once defended the principles of Paine's *Rights of Man*; had condemned the crusade against the Revolution as a great national crime; and, so far from being orthodox, had been described by his intimate friend, Coleridge, as a ' semi-atheist.' How was this brand snatched from the burning, or what, as others will say, led to this lamentable apostasy? There is, of course, no question of moral blame. As Browning observes, the real

[1] See Wordsworth's poem upon *Dion,* written 1816.

[2] *Le Général Michel Beaupuy.* Par G. Buissières et Émile Legouis. Paris, 1891.

Wordsworth was certainly not seduced by a 'bit of ribbon.' His change of attitude only suggested in a general way the theme of the poem. But a fair account of the way in which his change actually came about is interesting, both as explaining some of his literary tendencies and as illustrating a similar change in many of his contemporaries. Such an account may naturally be sought in Wordsworth's autobiographical poem, the *Prelude*, and there, indeed, it is implicitly given. Yet its significance is brought out by M. Legouis's careful study of the poem in connection with other documents and some of the earlier writings. M. Legouis has, I think, thrown new light upon the whole process; and in what I have to say I shall be mainly following his lead, though I may be making a slightly different estimate of certain elements of the question.

The *Prelude*, though it gives the clue, has one characteristic which obscures the self-revelation. Wordsworth describes facts till some of his readers are sick of them. Still, a fact is for him mainly a peg upon which to hang some poetical or philosophical conclusion. When, for example, he is crossing the Simplon, he supposes

—rather oddly, it seems to an Alpine traveller—
that the path is inviting him to ' ascend a lofty
mountain.' A peasant, luckily, informs him that
he has crossed the Alps already, and must go down
hill thenceforwards. This remark does not (in
the poem at least) suggest a prospect of dinner,
but a series of reflections upon ' that awful power'
Imagination. It convinces, or reminds, him that
' our being's' heart and home

> Is with infinitude and only there.

When a trivial incident starts a man at once upon
such distant reveries, serving as a mere taking-off
place for a flight into the clouds, we see that we
must not count upon definite, concrete information. We pass at a bound from the common
earth into a world lying beyond political or
historical circumstance. Even when he speaks,
not of external facts, but of the history of his own
opinions, he generally plunges into generalities so
wide that their precise application is not very easy
to discover. We can see that Wordsworth was
deeply moved by the Revolution, but the reflections stirred in him are beyond, or beneath, any
tangible political issue. They seem at first sight
as if they might be adopted with equal facility

by men of all political creeds. If a man tells
us that morality is, on the whole, a good thing,
we cannot infer whether he thinks this or that
political institution moral. Between the general
truth and the particular application there are
certain 'middle axioms' which Wordsworth
leaves us to supply for ourselves. And, in fact,
to follow his sentiments about the Revolution, we
must fill in a good deal that is not directly
stated. The generalities have to be clothed in
circumstance.

To understand Wordsworth himself we must
seek to reproduce him in the concrete. What
manner of man was this youth in the first flush
of enthusiasm? Wordsworth tells us how he
came to Cambridge, 'and at The Hoop alighted,
famous inn!' We can guess pretty well how
the freshman then impressed his tutor, or the
'chattering popinjays' whom men called fellow-
commoners. He was, he says, a 'stripling of the
hills, a Northern villager,' and probably uncouth
enough, even in the powdered hair and silk
stockings which he commemorates. The type
is familiar to all Cambridge men. Paley and
Bishop Watson had represented it in the previous
generation. A long procession of hard-headed

North-countrymen came up from the grammar-
schools of their district, and were among the
toughest competitors in the tripos.   Wordsworth,
no doubt, looked like a senior wrangler in
embryo.   He had not, indeed, the special taste
for mathematics.   There is an entry, it is said,
in one of the Cambridge registers about a youth
who applied for admission : *sed, Euclide viso,
cohorruit et evasit.*   Wordsworth did not precisely adopt that course; but he neglected his
Euclid, and took to learning Italian and reading
Spenser.   His poetical genius, however, was not
revealed to others, and not shown by the ordinary
symptoms.   He was not, like Coleridge, who was
to follow him to Cambridge, sensitive, emotional,
and sentimental.   However strong his feelings,
he was stern and little given to expansive
utterance.   He formed no intimate friendships.
Proud independence and power of standing on
his own sturdy legs would be his most conspicuous qualities, and went naturally with the
outside of a country bumpkin.   His boyhood
had stimulated these tendencies.   He had been
happy at his school at Hawkshead, and had
found congenial masters ; but their great merit
had been that they had cared nothing for modern

methods of drill and competition. They had left
him free to take long rambles over the fells,
scampers upon ponies, birds'-nesting expeditions,
and skating parties on the frozen lakes. He had
neither been trimmed into a model boy nor forced
into rebellion, but had grown up after his own
fashion. The early deaths of his parents had
thrown him still more upon his own resources,
and detached him from any close domestic ties.
Every Englishman is an island, it is said, and
Wordsworth was thoroughly insular or self-
contained by temperament and circumstance.
On the other hand, he was in thorough harmony
with his social surroundings. He was on the
friendliest terms with the old mistress of the
dame-school, the 'statesmen,' and the country
parsons of the district, whom he has idealised
in his poetry. Wordsworth, in short, was as
thorough a representative of the Cumbrian type
as Scott of the Scottish borderers, though with
a characteristic difference. He never cared, as
he remarks in the *Prelude*, for history or tradition. While Scott's memory had recorded every
legend and song connected with his beloved hills,
Wordsworth was curiously indifferent to all the
charm of historical association. He loved the

lakes and mountains, it might seem, for their
own sakes, not for the local heroes whose fame
was accidentally connected with them.   But he
had not the less imbibed the spirit of his own
district ; and loved the Pillar or Scawfell, if not
as the scene of any particular events, yet as the
natural guardian of the social order from which
he sprang.   This, again, had predisposed him to
a kind of old-fashioned republicanism.   At this
period, indeed, he was still unconscious of the
true nature of his own feelings.   He thought,
he says, at this time of nature, not of man.   But
he tells us, too, how when he went to France he
was a republican already, because he had been
brought up in a homely district where he had
never seen a man of rank or wealth, and how,
even at Cambridge, with all its faults, he had
found a community in which men were respected
for their own character and abilities, and all
' scholars and gentlemen' regarded as equals.
At Cambridge, it is true, Wordsworth seems to
have been amused rather than edified by the dons
of his time, the queer old humorists and port
wine drinking bachelors, who ought to have been
described by Charles Lamb.   Wordsworth passes
them by, observing only that he compared them

—with what results does not appear—to his own
'shepherd swains.' M. Legouis has formed a
low—I am afraid not too low—estimate of the
intellectual position of Cambridge in those days.
It may, however, be noticed that there was a
certain stir in the minds of its inhabitants even
then; Cambridge held itself to be the Whig
university, studying Locke and despising the
Aristotelian logic of Oxford. One symptom
was the development of certain free-thinking
tendencies, and the proceedings against Frend
for avowing Unitarianism were rousing an excitement which soon afterwards led Coleridge
into some trouble. Young men, therefore, who
aimed at enlightenment, as clever young men
ought to do, were not without temptations to
break bounds. Especially the uncouth young
Cumberland student,

> Child of the mountains, among shepherds reared,

despising the stupid old dons with their mechanical
disciplines, conscious of great abilities, though not
yet conscious of their proper aim, was disposed to
cast the dust off his shoes and strike out a path of
his own.

What it was to be, did not appear for some time.

His unsympathetic guardians naturally wanted him to settle to a profession, and their desire.was, if anything, a reason for going against it. To become a clergyman or a tutor was his only apparent chance, and yet either position involved concession, if not absolute subservience, to commonplaces and respectability. For some years, accordingly, Wordsworth lived what he calls an 'undomestic wanderer's life.' Travelling was congenial to his state of mind. A youth rambling with a knapsack on his back and a few pounds in his pocket can enjoy a sense of independence of the most exquisitely delightful kind. Wordsworth, before leaving Cambridge, had managed a tour in the Alps, and afterwards spent some time in London. He was equally in both cases a looker-on. The Swiss tour prompted a poem which (with the previous *Evening Walk*) shows that he was still in search of himself. He already shows his minute and first-hand observance of nature, but the form and the sentiment are imitative and partly fictitious. He is working the vein of Beattie's *Minstrel* and Goldsmith's *Traveller* ; with some impulse, perhaps, from Rousseau. M. Legouis observes very truly that the sentimental sadness which he thinks proper to affect is in odd contrast with the hearty

enjoyment betrayed in a letter of the same period
to his sister.   The Swiss tour took him through
France during the early enthusiasm of the Revolution, and his sympathy was the natural expansion
of the crude republicanism of the Cumberland shepherd and Cambridge undergraduate.   His London
experience is characteristic.   He is essentially the
countryman wondering at the metropolis.   In the
seventh book of the *Prelude* he gives a list of all
the sights which bewildered him, from Burke in
the House of Commons and Mrs. Siddons on the
stage, down to waxworks and blind beggars in the
streets and shameless women using bad language
in public-houses.   He passes from his quaint bits of
prose—unconsciously humorous—to pathetic and
elevating thoughts.   But the spectacle passes before
him without involving him ; he has no talks,
like Coleridge's, at the Cat and Salutation to
record ; he picks up no chums and joins no clubs ;
his proper position is that of the famous sonnet on
Westminster Bridge, when he alone wakes and
meditates on the ' mighty heart ' that is ' lying still.'
London is part of that vast machinery, including
the universe in general, of which it sometimes
seems to be the final cause that it is to mould the
central object, William Wordsworth.   It suggests

to him, for a wonder, that there are other people in the world besides himself.   It impresses upon him, in his own words, 'the unity of man.'   As he approaches on his 'itinerant vehicle'—a coach, to wit—'a weight of ages' descends at once upon 'his heart.'   He becomes aware, shall we say, that, besides the mountains and the lakes, there is a vast drama of human joy and suffering constantly developing itself, and that, though he still looks upon it from the outside, it means a great process in which he is to play his part—if only he can find his appropriate function.

This brings us to Wordsworth's important visit to France in 1791.   He went there, it seems, on some vague pretext that a knowledge of the language might qualify him for a tutorship.   His re-volutionary fervour was still comparatively mild. He picked up a stone on the site of the Bastille, 'in guise of an enthusiast,' but 'in honest truth,' he affected 'more emotion than he felt,' and was more moved by the sight of Le Brun's 'Magdalene' than by relics of the great events.   Passing on to Orléans, however, he made acquaintance with some officers, and among them with Beaupuy, upon whom his comrades of royalist sympathies turned a cold shoulder.   Wordsworth soon attached himself to Beaupuy, and one main secret of their sympathy is revealed in an anecdote. They met a ' hunger-bitten girl' leading a heifer by a cord tied to her arm, while she was 'knitting in a heartless mood of solitude.' 'Tis against that that we are fighting,' said his friend. Wordsworth took the Revolution to mean the destruction of 'abject poverty' by the abolition of exclusive privileges and the elevation of human beings intrusted with power over their own lives. He caught the contagion of the patriotic enthusiasm with which the French rose to meet their invaders in 1792. He became so hearty a sympathiser that he was almost inclined to join in some active movement, and might, he remarks, have ended his career by the guillotine. He was forced, probably by stress of money, to return to England, passing through Paris soon after the September massacres; and might have said afterwards, as Bolingbroke said to Atterbury, that he was being exchanged for Paine, who had just crossed in the opposite direction.

So far Wordsworth's case was not peculiar. He shared the sentiments of most generous and intelligent young men at the dawn of a new era.

Bliss was it at that time to be alive,
But to be young was very Heaven!

He had not to part from early convictions, but simply to develop his old feelings : to diffuse more widely, as he puts it, the affections which had 'grown up with him from the cradle.' His ready-made republicanism did not clash as yet with his patriotism. Rather the two principles were in harmony. The good old conviction that Britons never would be slaves like the wretched beings who wore wooden shoes and had never heard of trial by jury, was enough to bear him out. It only wanted to be mellowed by a little philosophy and wider humanity. The poor girl towing her heifer was to be raised to the level of the hearty young Cumberland lasses with whom he had danced and flirted. The clumsy story of *Vaudracour and Julia*, derived, it seems, from Beaupuy's illustrations of the arbitrary tyranny of the French *noblesse*, could be told without suggesting any English parallel. It is true that Wordsworth had realised in the case of Lord Lowther how difficult it might be to force a great English noble to pay his just debts. But even Lord Lowther could not imprison his dependants by a *lettre de cachet* or make Cumberland peasants pay crushing taxes and flog the meres at night to silence the frogs. All that was

wanted at home was to put down jobbery and
rotten boroughs; and if reform was desired, there
was not in Wordsworth's class at any rate any
accumulated mass of palpable tyranny to give
rancour to the demand, or mingle it with a thirst
for revenge. The Whiggism of Fox or Sheridan,
in his view as in theirs, implied sympathy with
the French Revolution, so long as the Revolution
could be regarded merely as an application of
Mr. Locke's principles and a copy of our glorious
achievement of 1688.

Wordsworth, however, had to discover, like
his contemporaries, that the millennium was not to
come so cheaply. The English war with France
and the Reign of Terror in France roused a painful
conflict of feeling. It has been suggested that
Wordsworth was alienated from the Revolution,
not by the horrors of 1793, but by his patriotic
sentiment. He could pardon the Jacobins for
their crimes in France, but not for opposing
British interests. A closer observation shows
that this partly misrepresents the facts. The war,
indeed, as Wordsworth tells us, first broke up
his placid optimism. He was in the Isle of
Wight in 1793, listened with painful forebodings
to the sunset gun, and watched the fleet gather-

ing to join in 'the unworthy service' of suppressing liberty abroad. He even 'exulted,' he
tells us, when the first attempts of Englishmen
to resist the revolutionary armies met with shame-
ful defeat; and sat gloomily in church when
prayers were offered for victory, feeding on the
day of vengeance yet to come. Some people
were cosmopolitan enough to find no difficulty in
suppressing patriotic compunctions ; but Wordsworth, solitary and recluse as he was, was pene-
trated to the core by the sentiments of which
patriotism is the natural growth. He only, he
says, who 'loves the sight of a village steeple as I
do' can judge of 'the conflict of sensations without
name' with which he joined such congregations.
His private and public sympathies were now
clashing in the cruelest way. Meanwhile, he felt
the taunts of those who were echoing Madame
Roland's cry, 'O liberty, what crimes are committed in thy name !' It was well that the
infant republic had 'throttled the snakes about its
cradle' with the might of a Hercules; but his
soul was sick at thought of the odium that was
being incurred by liberty. His thoughts by day
were 'most melancholy,' and 'for months and
years, after the last beat of those atrocities,' he

could not sleep without hideous nightmares of cruel massacre and vain pleadings in unjust tribunals. The argument from atrocities, however, though the most popular, was ambiguous. Wordsworth had been profoundly affected by the September massacres when passing through Paris on his return; but he could still argue that such crimes were the natural fruit of the ignorance and misery of the people under the old system, and that when the wretches who had seized upon power were suppressed, the true reign of peace and reason would begin. The hope seemed to be justified by the fall of Robespierre (July 1794), and Wordsworth describes minutely how he heard the news in Morecambe Bay; what ecstasy it caused him, and how he now called upon the ' golden times' to appear. It became sufficiently clear, however, that, whatever else was to happen, the new rulers of France were not to be pure philanthropists, propagating a gospel of humanity by peaceful means. The French, he began to fear, were changing a war of self-defence for one of conquest. Yet he stuck resolutely to his opinions as long as he could. He adhered ' more firmly to old tenets'—that is, to his revolutionary creed — tried to ' hide the wounds of mortified presumption,' and, in fact, had to construct a theory to show that he had been right all along. Such theories are essential to one's comfort, but sometimes troublesome to construct. 'Opinions,' as he put it, grew 'into consequence,' and for instinctive sympathy he wished to substitute a reasoned system of principles.

Wordsworth was thus set down to a problem, and his solution was characteristic. In such mental crises the real process of decision is often very different from that of which the subject of the process is himself conscious. He fancies, in all sincerity, that he is considering a logical or philosophical question. He is asking whether reason, impartially consulted, will order him to accept one or the other of two conflicting systems ; though hoping that it will enable him to decide at the smallest possible cost to his belief in his own consistency. He would prefer a theory which would enable him to think that the opinions which he has to abandon represent a merely superficial aberration. But this may practically come to asking what are his own strongest feelings, and assuming that they represent eternal truths. Wordsworth supposed him-

self to be asking simply, What is the true philosophy of the political creeds at issue? He was
unconsciously asking, On what side are my really
deepest sympathies? The last question might
be put thus : A Cumberland 'statesman' could
develop into a Girondin (or what he took to be
a Girondin) by simply widening his sympathies.
That might be a case of natural development,
involving no shock or laceration of old ties; but,
could he continue the process and grow into
a Jacobin? That involved a strain upon his
patriotism, painful but not absolutely coercive.
He could manage to desire the defeat of British
armies, and all the more readily when the
British Government was alienating him by trying
to suppress freedom of thought and language
at home. Still, this position required an effort ;
and another trial was behind it. Could the
'statesman' sympathise with men who used such
weapons as massacre and the guillotine? To
that, of course, there could be only one answer—
Wordsworth had been wayward and independent, but never a rebel against society or morality.
He was thoroughly in harmony with the simple,
homely society from which he sprang. Violence
and confiscation were abhorrent to him. 'I recoil,'

he tells a friend at the time, 'from the very
idea of a revolution. I am a determined enemy
to every species of violence.' Lord Lowther,
let us say, should be made to pay his debts and
give up his boroughs ; but he certainly should
not have his head placed on the walls of Car-
lisle, while his estates were divided among the
peasantry. Wordsworth, however, could still hope
that the Terrorists were a passing phenomenon,
an 'ephemeral monster,' as he puts it ; and was
still firmly persuaded of this upon the fall of
Robespierre. It was, however, essential to his
peace of mind that the facts should confirm this
view : and that the French people, freed from
the incubus, should show themselves clearly in
favour of peaceful progress at home, and free
from thought of conquest abroad.

The mental crisis thus brought about is indicated by some remarkable writings. Wordsworth
had been provoked to an utterance of his sentiments when the English declaration of war was
stimulating his wrath. Watson — who, being
Bishop of Llandaff and Professor of Divinity at
Cambridge, passed his time as an intelligent
country gentleman at Windermere—had preached
the doctrine that every Englishman should be

thoroughly contented with his lot. They could not all be non-resident bishops, but they had no grievances to speak of. Wordsworth hereupon wrote a letter in which he is, at least, unmistakably on the side of Paine against Burke. He had at this time adopted the opinions of Beaupuy. He objects on principle to monarchy and to privileged orders of nobility. At most it may be said that his argument is not so much that of the theorist arguing from abstract rights, as of the independent Briton who will not humble himself to a lord, and whose republicanism resembles Milton's rather than Rousseau's. But now, when he was roused by later developments to look into his first principles, he found himself in a cruel difficulty. In the first place, Wordsworth, though he was a philosophical poet, was not at home in metaphysical or logical subtleties. He is the antithesis of Coleridge, who combined in so singular a degree the poetical and the reasoning faculties. Coleridge could keep the two faculties apart; and his poems—the really exquisite poems, at least—are as free from any admixture of philosophy as if he had never heard of 'object' and 'subject.' The cause of the difference is simple, namely, that Wordsworth's philosophy, such as it is, represents intuitions or convictions; it embodies his faith as to the world and human nature, without reference to the logical justifications.   Coleridge held, as a metaphysician naturally does, that his philosophic creed required to be justified by a whole apparatus of dialectics which would be out of place in verse.   Whether this apparatus was really the base of his convictions, or represents the after-thought by which he justified them, does not matter.   Wordsworth, in any case, is content to expound his philosophy as self-evident.   He speaks as from inspiration, not as the builder of a logical system.   One result was that when he tried to argue, he got, as he admits with his usual *naïveté*, 'endlessly perplexed' (p. 307).   He wanted 'formal proof,' and could not find it.   He did not, of course, join the 'scoffers'; a sufficient reason was, as the scoffers would say, that he was incompetent to appreciate them.   When, in the *Excursion*, he audaciously calls Voltaire 'dull,' he is tacitly admitting that he could never see a joke.   Anyhow, after bothering himself with metaphysics till his head turned, he fortunately resolved to be a poet; and here had a short cut to his conclusions.   I do not mean to scoff at Wordsworth.

My own belief is that he took more simply
and openly the path which most of us take, and
that impartial inquiry with him, as with nearly
every one, meant simply discovering what he had
really thought all along.

Another influence must be noticed here.   M.
Legouis dwells upon Wordsworth's relations to
Godwin.   There is not much direct evidence
upon this matter ; and I have some doubt whether
M. Legouis does not rather overstate the case.
But, in the main, I think that he is substantially
right.   That is to say, when Wordsworth set about
what he called thinking, I suppose that Godwin's
philosophy would represent political theory for him.
Godwin's philosophy was transmuted by Shelley
into something very exquisite if rather nonsensical,
and probably is now remembered, when remembered at all, chiefly for that reason.   Hazlitt,
however, in his slashing way tells us that Godwin
was at this period the ' very god of our idolatry ' ;
Tom Paine was considered for a time a fool to
him ; Paley an old woman ; Edmund Burke 'a
flashy sophist' (*Spirit of the Age*, p. 33).   Wordsworth, in particular, he adds, told a student to
' throw aside his books of chemistry and read
Godwin on Necessity ' !   Both Wordsworth and

Coleridge were in various ways connected with the Godwin circle. Now, Godwinism, presented as the gospel of the Revolution, indicates Wordsworth's difficulty with curious precision. Godwin, of course, appeals to Reason, and in general terms Wordsworth, like every one on his side of the question, agreed. Their essential aim was to get rid of superstition and obsolete tradition. Godwin, too, held Reason to be a peaceable goddess, whose only weapon was persuasion, not force. Godwin never erred from excess of passion, and was by no means the kind of wood of which martyrs or fanatics are made. Man, he thought, was perfectible, and a little calm argument would make him perfect. So far Wordsworth might agree during his early enthusiasm. The people, freed from the domination of their false guides, were to come to their senses and establish the reign of peace and liberty. But Godwin went a step further. Reason, according to him, leads straight to anarchy. Rulers, of course, will not be wanted when men are perfectly reasonable. But, moreover, rules in general will not be wanted. Men will not tie their hands by custom or prejudice. They will act in each case for the best, that is, for the

happiness of the greatest number, without slavery
to formulas.   His political ideal is, therefore,
individualism, or atomism ; the doctrine of liberty
raised to the highest terms.   Thus, for example,
marriage is an absurdity.   If two people agree to
live together, they are 'unreasonable' to enslave
themselves to a tie which may become irksome.
They should be free to part at any moment.
Society should be nothing but an aggregate of
independent units, bound together by no rules
whatever.   A rule should never survive its
reason, and the only reason for a rule is the
calculation that it will make us happy.

The doctrine had an apparent consistency, at
least, which served to show Wordsworth whither
he was going.   Two curious poems of this period
illustrate his feelings.   After leaving the Isle of
Wight, Wordsworth had rambled over Salisbury
Plain and been profoundly impressed by the
scenery.   There, too, he had apparently heard the
story which is told in one of the last *Ingoldsby
Legends*.   In 1786,[1] one Jarvis Matcham had
been startled by a thunderstorm, and confessed to
a companion that he had committed a murder

---

[1] The story, which Barham says came to him from Sir Walter
Scott, is told in the *New Annual Register* for 1786.

('scuttled a poor little drummer-boy's nob,' as
Barham puts it) some years before. In Wordsworth's version, the murderer is not a 'bloodthirsty swab,' but an amiable person, who 'would
not have robbed the raven of its food.' He had
been seized by a press-gang, and, finding on his
return that his family were in distress, had robbed
and murdered a miscellaneous traveller for their
benefit; an act possibly excusable on Godwin's
principles. With this story Wordsworth combined another of the 'female vagrant,' whose
cruel sufferings were due to her husband having
been forced into the army. This represents, as
he tells us, foreboding thoughts which came to
him when watching the British Fleet at Spithead.
He foresaw that the war was leading to 'misery
beyond all possible calculation.' Wretched men
were being forcibly torn from their families, and
plunged not only into misery, but into crime.
The horrors of war are bad enough, but they
involve also a difficult moral problem when the
victims not only suffer, but are demoralised : and
painful forebodings were combined with bewilder-
ment as to ethical puzzles. Was the murderer
most to blame, or the tyrants who had crushed his
life? and what are we to think of the Providential

government under which such things are possible and even natural? The moral problem is more prominent in the curious tragedy, *The Borderers.* That tragedy, received with rapture by his new friend, Coleridge, was written, he says, to be read, not to be acted; and, like most tragedies so written, has almost failed to find readers, as it quite failed to find actors. Had he written it later, he says, he should have introduced a more complex plot and a greater variety of characters. He might have tried; but nobody could have a less dramatic genius than Wordsworth, who could never describe any character except his own. *The Borderers*, however, is noticeable here only as an illustration of his state of mind. It was meant to embody a theory, upon which at the time he wrote a prose essay, namely, how we are to explain the 'apparently motiveless actions of bad men.' His villain is a man who erroneously supposed that he was joining in an act of justice when he was really becoming accomplice in an atrocious crime. Having found out his mistake, he resolves, not to repent, but in future to commit any number of crimes on his own account. Conscience is a nuisance and remorse a mistake. The villain not only acts upon his principles, but endeavours to subject the hero of the piece to a similar process of conversion. The hero, in fact, is induced by his machinations to cause the death of a virtuous old gentleman, under specially atrocious circumstances. The villain calculates that, having thus become an unconscious sinner, the hero will in future be a systematic and deliberate sinner, and a convenient subordinate. I do not feel much clearer, I confess, as to apparently motiveless actions after reading the play than before. The villain's sophistry does not strike me as very plausible, nor his motives, on his own showing, as very intelligible. Wordsworth's own state of mind, however, is clearer. He had, he says, seen many such cases during the advance of the French Revolutionists 'to the extreme of wickedness.' Men are led into crime from originally good motives, and there is then no limit to the consequent 'hardening of the heart and perversion of the understanding.' Robespierre, whose fall had rejoiced him, had started from most benevolent principles, and ended by becoming the typical monster. The temporary success, too, of the villainy, and the perversion of power granted in the name of human liberty to a crushing and bloodthirsty tyranny, were bewildering. 'Often,' says Coleridge in *The Friend*, 'have I reflected with awe on the great and disproportionate power which an individual of no extraordinary talents or attainments may exert, by merely throwing off all restraints of conscience.'   And what, he adds, must not be the power of an individual of consummate wickedness who can organise all the forces of a nation?   Robespierre, or Napoleon, would have found conscience a great impediment; Godwin's theory seemed to Wordsworth to make it superfluous.   Godwin would suppress conscience, and substitute calculation.   No doubt for him the calculation was to include the happiness of all. Only, when you have suppressed all ties and associations, it becomes rather puzzling to say what reason you have for caring for others.   If husbands and wives may part when it is agreeable to both, will they not part when it is agreeable to either?   If a statesman may break through all laws when they oppose a useful end, will he not most simply define useful as useful to himself? Take leave, in other words, of all prejudices and all respect for social bonds, and are you not on the high road to become such a one as the villain of *The Borderers*?   These are, in fact, the problems which Wordsworth tells us brought him into endless perplexity. What, after all, was the meaning of right and wrong, and obligation? (p. 307). What was the lordly 'attribute' of freewill but a mockery, if we have neither any real knowledge of what will do good, nor of why we should do it? He could, he says, 'unsoul by syllogistic words' the 'mysteries of being' which make 'of the whole human race one brotherhood.' It was in the name of the brotherhood that the revolutionary teachers appealed to him; and yet Godwin, as a prophet, ended by dissolving all society into a set of unconnected atoms. M. Legouis remarks that Wordsworth 'purged himself of his pessimism' after the fashion of Goethe, by putting it into a book. This, however, must not be taken to imply that Wordsworth ever shared the atrocious sentiments of his imaginary villain. *The Borderers* naturally recalls Schiller's *Robbers*, which had just been translated, and was not without influence upon Wordsworth. Wordsworth's villain and hero are contrasted much as Schiller's two Moors. But it could never have been expected that any young Englishman would, like the alleged German baron, have taken to the highway to realise Wordsworth's imaginary personages. *The Borderers* is not only

without the imaginative vigour which at the time
made Schiller's bombast excusable—-the product
of a contemplative speculation instead of youthful
passion,—but it is plain enough that the poet
loathes his villain too much to allow him the least
attractiveness.   The play represents the kind of
moral spasm by which a man repels a totally uncongenial element of thought.   He had found
that what he took for a wholesome food contained
a deadly poison, and to become conscious of its
nature is to expel it with disgust.

What was the influence, then, which opened
Wordsworth's eyes and caused what seemed, at
least, to be a change of front?   He answers that
question himself by referring to two influences.
The first was the influence of the devoted sister
who now came to live with him.   She pointed out
to him that his 'office upon earth' was to be a
poet.   She persuaded him, one may say, to cease
to bother himself with Godwin's metaphysics, with
puzzles as to Freewill and Necessity and the
ground of moral obligation, and to return to his
early aspirations.   If this bit of advice fell in with
his own predisposition, the influence of Dorothy
Wordsworth was something far more than could
be summed up in any advice, however judicious.

It meant, in brief, that Wordsworth had by his side a woman of high enthusiasm and cognate genius, thoroughly devoted to him and capable of sharing his inspiration; and that thus the 'undomestic wanderer' was to be bound by one of the sweetest and purest of human ties. His early affections, hitherto deprived of any outlet, could now revive, and his profound sense of their infinite value encouraged him to break the chains of logic, or rather to set down the logic as sophistry. Godwinism meant a direct assault upon the family tie; and that tie was now revealing its value by direct experience of its power. The friendship with Coleridge, then in the full flush of youthful genius, and the most delightful and generous of admirers, came to encourage the growth of such feelings; while Coleridge's mystical tendencies in philosophy probably suggested some solution of the Godwin 'syllogising.' Perhaps, after all, Godwin might be a humbug, and the true key to the great problems was to be found in Germany, where both the young men were soon to go for initiation. Meanwhile, however, another influence was affecting Wordsworth. His sister had led him back to nature, and he now found that nature

should include the unsophisticated human being.
He rambled as of old, and in his rambles found
that the 'lonely roads were open schools' in
which he might study the passions and thoughts
of unsophisticated human beings.   The result
was remarkable.   He found nobility and sense
in the humble friends.   The 'wealthy few' see
by 'artificial lights,' and 'neglect the universal
heart.'   Nature is equally corrupted in the 'close
and overcrowded haunts of cities.'   But in the
poor men, who reminded him of his early friends,
of the schoolmaster 'Matthew,' and old Dame
Tyson, he found the voice of the real man ; and
observed 'how oft high service is performed
within' men's hearts which resemble not pompous
temples, but the 'mere mountain chapel.'   Was
not this to go back to Rousseau, to denunciations
of luxury and exaltations of the man of nature?
Wordsworth had been converted to the Revolution
by the sight of the poor peasant girl, the victim
of feudal privileges—why should he renounce the
Revolution by force of sympathy with the same
class in England?

Before answering, I may remark that in any
case the impression was deep and lasting.   It shows
how Wordsworth reached his famous theory that

the language of poetry should be indistinguishable from that of ordinary life. That is merely the literary translation of his social doctrine. He and Coleridge have both told us how they agreed to divide labour, and, while Coleridge was to give human interest to the romantic, Wordsworth was to show the romance which is incorporated in commonplace things. Wordsworth proceeded to write the poems which appeared in the *Lyrical Ballads* ; and, if his theory tripped him up sometimes, wrote some of those exquisite and pathetic passages which amply redeem intervening tracts of quaintly prosaic narrative and commonplace moralising—some of the passages, in short, which make one love Wordsworth, and feel his unequalled power of soothing and humanising sorrow. *Simon Lee*—to mention only one—was the portrait of an old man at Alfoxden. If you are apt to yawn in the middle, you recognise the true Wordsworth at the conclusion :

> I 've heard of hearts unkind, kind deeds
>   With coldness still returning;
> Alas! the gratitude of man
>   Hath oftener left me mourning!

I must not, however, speak of Wordsworth's

pathetic power, which, in its way, seems to me to
be unapproachable. Henceforward, he found in
such themes the inspiration of his truest poetry.
The principle is given in the *Song at the Feast at
Brougham Castle,* where he says of the shepherd
lord :

> Love had he found in huts where poor men lie,
> His daily teachers had been fields and rills,

and in countless other utterances of the same
sentiment. A change, indeed, took place, of
which M. Legouis gives a curious illustration.
About the beginning of 1798, Wordsworth, as he
shows, wrote the story of the ruined cottage which
is now imbedded in the fifth book of the *Excursion.*
M. Legouis translates the story, omitting the
subsequent interpolations. Coleridge, long afterwards, declared it to be the finest poem of the
same length in our language. The poem, as
originally written, is a painfully pathetic story of
undeserved misery patiently borne, and ending in
the destruction of a peasant's household. In the
later form the narrator has to interrupt himself by
apologies for the sadness of the story and edifying
remarks upon the ways of Providence. Wordsworth, somehow or other, had become reconciled.

The change was not the abandonment of his old sentiments, but the indication that they were again coming to the surface and casting off a heterogeneous element. The superficial change, indeed, was marked enough. To Wordsworth, the revolutionary movement now represented not progress —the natural expansion of his sympathies—but social disintegration and the attack upon all that he held to be the most valuable. The secret is revealed by his remarkable letter to Fox in 1801. There he calls the statesman's attention to two of his most significant poems, *The Brothers* and *Michael*. These poems are intended to describe the domestic affections ' as they exist among a class of men now almost confined to the North of England.' He observes that the little holdings of the ' statesmen ' serve to strengthen the family tie, and thus protect a ' fountain of affection pure as his heart was intended for.' This class, he adds, is rapidly disappearing, and its disappearance indicates the greatest of our national dangers. These most touching poems, written in 1800, represent Wordsworth's final solution of his problem, and embody a sentiment which runs through his later work. Its meaning is clear enough. Wordsworth had begun to feel that Godwin's anti-social logic had an embodiment in facts. What he now saw behind it was not Rousseau's sentimentalism, but the harsh doctrinaire system of the economists. The theorists who professed to start from the rights of man were really attacking the essential social duties. Godwinism meant the 'individualism' of the later economists. Individualism meant the reckless competition and race for wealth which were destroying the very framework of peaceful society. The English Radical represented Adam Smith; and Wordsworth now perceived

> How dire a thing,
> Is worshipped in that idol, proudly named
> The 'Wealth of Nations.'

The evils which now impressed him were the absorption of small freeholds by large estates, and the growth of the factory system in the place of domestic manufacture. He dwells upon these evils in the *Excursion* in language which gives a foretaste of much modern Socialism. Wordsworth had plenty of allies in this view of the case. While he was renouncing the principle of Individualism, Owen was beginning to put in practice the

schemes suggested by the same evils, and leading
to his later Socialism.   Cobbett was lamenting the
demoralisation of the agricultural labourer, and
taking up his curious position of Radicalism inspired by regret for the 'good old times.'   There
is no need, at the present day, for expounding
such views or explaining why it should appear to
Wordsworth that the revolutionary movement
which had started by taking up the cause of the
poor had ended by assailing the very basis of
order and morality.   The foreign developments,
the growth of a military despotism, and the
oppression of Switzerland by France in the name
of fraternity, no doubt seemed clear justifications
of his attitude.   But he had sufficient reasons at
home.   The Radical, with whom he had been allied,
was attacking what he held dearest,—not only
destroying the privileges of nobles, but breaking
up the poor man's home, and creating a vast 'pro-
letariat'—a mass of degraded humanity—instead
of encouraging 'plain living and high thinking,'
and destroying the classes whose simplicity and
independence had made them the soundest element
of mutual prosperity.   I do not, of course, inquire
how far Wordsworth's estimate of the situation

was sound.   I only say that this explains how he
reached it naturally and consistently.   It was, as I
have said, anything but a purely logical process,
though it may be said that it was guided by an
implicit logic.   It really meant that he became
aware of the fact that his instincts had led him into
the camp of his real enemies.   When he realised
the fact, he stuck to his instincts, and, indeed, regarded them as due to divine inspiration.   They
were attacked by the revolutionary party.   He
would find in them not only the source of happiness, but the ultimate revelation of religion and
morality :

> The primal duties shine aloft like stars ;
> The charities that soothe and heal and bless
> Are scattered at the feet of men like flowers.

Wordsworth's ultimate doctrine, one may say,
is the duty of cherishing the 'intimations of immortality' which visit our infancy, to transmute
sorrow into purifying and strengthening influence:
and so to 'build up our moral being.'   In his
particular case, this, no doubt, meant that the boy
of Hawkshead was to be the father of the man who
could not be permanently held by the logical toils
of Godwin.   It meant, too, a certain self-com-

placency and an optimistic tendency which, however pleasant, dulled his poetic fervour, and made
him acquiesce in much that he would once have
rejected.   But it was also the source of a power
which should be recognised by men of a different
belief.   When J. S. Mill went through the mental
crisis described in his *Autobiography*, he thought
that he had injured his powers of feeling by the
habit of constant analysis.   He had so destroyed
the associations and with them the sympathies
which make life desirable.   In this state of mind
he found an admirable restorative in Wordsworth's
poetry.   'Analysis' represents just the intellectual
habit which Wordsworth denounces.   It is the
state of mind in which his imaginary man of science
botanises on his mother's grave ; picks the flowers
to pieces and drops the sentiment.   Mill, accordingly, tried and tried, he says, successfully,
to adopt Wordsworth's method ; and to find
happiness in 'tranquil contemplation,' while yet
strengthening his interest in the 'common feelings
and common destiny of human beings.'   With
' culture of this sort,' he says, ' there was nothing to
dread from the most confirmed habit of analysis '
(146-9).   If Mill's great aim was to 'humanise'

political economy, he drew from Wordsworth encouragement for the task. This point of contact between two men, each of whom represents much that was most antipathetic to the other, is significant. It suggests much upon which I cannot dwell; but it may hint to the Radical that Wordsworth, in giving up a doctrine which he never really assimilated, was faithful to convictions which, partial or capable of perversion as they may be, represent a very important aspect of truth.

Printed by T. and A. CONSTABLE, Printers to Her Majesty
at the Edinburgh University Press

For EU product safety concerns, contact us at Calle de José Abascal, 56–1°,
28003 Madrid, Spain or eugpsr@cambridge.org.

www.ingramcontent.com/pod-product-compliance
Ingram Content Group UK Ltd.
Pitfield, Milton Keynes, MK11 3LW, UK
UKHW010344140625
459647UK00010B/820